MW01065546

GLIMPSES

Short Stories

Winfield Goulden

iUniverse, Inc.
New York Bloomington

GLIMPSES
Short Stories

Cover Art: "Horning In" - Sylvia Hamilton Goulden

iUniverse books may be ordered through booksellers or by contacting:

iUniverse
1663 Liberty Drive
Bloomington, IN 47403
www.iuniverse.com
1-800-Authors (1-800-288-4677)

Because of the dynamic nature of the Internet, any Web addresses or links contained in this book may have changed since publication and may no longer be valid.

ISBN: 978-1-4502-2939-5 (sc)
ISBN: 978-1-4502-2940-1 (ebk)

Printed in the United States of America

iUniverse rev. date: 7/28/2010

*This book is dedicated to James Frederick Thurman ~
my strongest supporter, my severest critic, and my best friend.*

Edited by Sylvia H. Goulden

Contents

THE GIRLS OF SUMMER. 1

PROM DATE. 5

JENNY. 9

BIRDLAND. 13

SPITFIRE. 17

DRUG STORE COWBOY 21

BUGLES. 25

HAIL CAESAR! 27

LOVE AFFAIR. 31

SLUMBER PARTY. 35

LADY DAY. 37

A GATHERING OF EAGLES. 41

GENESIS 43

52ND STREET 45

BABYFACE 51

LADY IN WAITING 55

BEWARE OF FOREIGN ENTANGLEMENTS. 61

BLOOD BROTHERS 65

CAFÉ DE LA PAIX 69

AVENUE OF THE STARS 73

HEAT. 77

AIR MAIL 79

DIALOGUE. 85

SUMMER STREET. 89

GREYLOCK REVISITED. 93

INTERMISSION RIFF 97

DOC 103

UNTITLED. 107

LITTLE OLD LADY FROM PASADENA 113

THE HOUSE ON THE HILL 117

FLIGHT THIRTEEN 121

WINTER DREAMS. 125

POISON IVY. 129

MILITARY INTELLIGENCE 133

DUKE'S MIXTURE 135

TWELVE 139

THE CAPTAIN AND THE SERGEANT 143

PEARL'S PEOPLE 147

SUNDAY 153

WEDDING PRESCENCE 157

SYLVIA. 161

STOMACH MUSCLES. 163

WINTER DREAMS II. 165

Glimpses

THE GIRLS OF SUMMER

When I went to sleep last night, I took a journey, drifting tranquilly through the world of long ago, when I was a teenager. In that dream, once again, I met Christine, and Helen, and Mary Lou, and Betty, and Blondie, and Hope and yes, there was a Beverly, too.

For *these* were the girls of summer.

We all lived in a small New England factory town, Stamford, Connecticut, located about 35 miles from New York City, population in 1934, about 30,000.

We all attended Stamford High School (colors: orange and black). Some of us, like me, were on the football team. Others were cheerleaders or members of the band. The girls filled the wooden, slatted grandstand for the home games at Halloween Park, sweltering in the early Autumn heat (we called it Indian Summer), and then freezing as late fall became winter and the bitter wind off Long Island Sound bit deeply into our bones.

It was then that the girls, stomping up and down in unison to keep warm, shouted this song which, in today's parlance, would be regarded as incredibly corny, but then we regarded it as incredibly 'cool'.

> *"Beer, beer for old Stamford High*
> *Shake up the cocktails*
> *Bring on the rye*
> *Send the freshman out for gin*
> *Don't let a sober sophomore in*
> *We stagger on*

But we never fall
We sober up
On wood alcohol
When we're drunk
We fight like hell
For the honor of Stamford High"

On Sundays, we went to the Methodist Church. It didn't matter that some were Catholic or Jewish – we just went. Why? Because the Methodist Church had:

1. A bowling alley in the basement
2. A basketball court one flight up
3. A young Pastor, barely out of Divinity School, with wildly progressive ideas about religious tolerance.
4. And last, but of prime importance, great back pews where we could cuddle with our individual girl friends while the gigantic pipe organ boomed encouragement.

Then after Sunday services were over, we headed down Main Street to Hatch's Ice Cream Parlor. There we probed the gooey delights of Hatch's Sunday Special. It was called, appropriately enough, a "Dusty Sundae".

Ingredients:
2 large scoops vanilla ice cream
Pour on chocolate sauce
Sprinkle with powdered malted milk
Cover with a dollop of fresh whipped cream
Garnish with Maraschino cherry
Price: 25 cents

Many was the time we boys would pool all our change, and when we came up short, we would feel the sweet breath of summer as the girls helped us out secretly under the table, slipping us a dime or a quarter to meet the bill.

When World War II devastated our town and all the boys went off to war and the bugles blared, the girls of summer were there for us:

They were there for us when Pearl Harbor was attacked.

They were there for us when they prayed for us at the Methodist Church, the Catholic Church and the Jewish Synagogue.

And when we died at places like Guadalcanal, Attu, Kiska, Normandy, Bastogne, Anzio, Cassino and Berlin, the girls of summer were there for us again. They followed in the wake of the Western Union boy on the bicycle who delivered that terrible laconic telegram:

"The Secretary of War regrets to inform you, your son Myron Mantell, killed in action, 6 June 1944 in Normandy, France."

They were there for us when they visited our bereaved parents and their families, and held them to their bosoms, sharing their grief. They brought food and little cakes of sympathy, remembrance and love.

And when it was *finally over*, we came marching back. And although the girls of summer greeted us warmly, it was *not* the same. It was *never* the same again.

The Methodist Church had been razed. Hatch's Ice Cream Parlor burned to the ground.

They were gone. And we were gone too; our faith; our naiveté; and our innocence.

Gone forever.

PROM DATE

I knocked timidly on the front door. There I stood, clad in a white double-breasted Palm Beach summer suit, dark blue shirt, white tie and white Cuban-heeled shoes. Clutched in my left hand was a box containing a gardenia corsage. My blond hair was slicked back, with the inevitable cowlick sticking straight up on the back of my head – a Norman Rockwell poster boy if there ever was one.

I was there to pick up my date, Miss Betty Murray, and take her to the high school Senior Prom.

The locale: Stamford Connecticut. The date: 1937. I was sixteen years old.

The door opened: "Good evening, Winfield."

"Hello, Mr. Murray."

"Come in, come in," he said with a smiling nod.

Mr. Murray was a known and respected man in our town, and, it was said that he was "somewhat well off," which meant, in those dark days of the Great Depression, that he had a job and a roof over his head. He was a small, almost fragile man with delicate features, balding, with a few wisps of grey hair left and he was clad in his usual velveteen smoking jacket. A white, starched shirt with a celluloid collar and a perfectly knotted black tie completed his ensemble. And, of course, a pair of glasses perched on the end of his nose.

He was a very formal man, who spoke in hushed tones as he showed me to a chair in the parlor. We sat down and began the following sparkling conversation:

"Would you like a glass of water, Winfield?"

"No, thank you, sir."

"I trust that your mother and father are well?"

"Yes, sir."

"And your two grandmothers and great grandmother?"

"Yes, sir."

"And your brother and sister, as well?"

"Yes, sir."

"Both of them?"

"Yes, sir."

I clutched the corsage box in my sweaty palms. I was beginning to squirm. "Oh," Mr. Murray said, as an afterthought, "Mrs. Murray advises me that our daughter Betty will be down shortly."

But now, I must digress – to tell you that the Murrays owned a dog. His name was Jupey. He was a British bulldog, with an ugly under shod jaw; not only that, he was an *old* British bulldog, given to terrible farts that were known to curl the wallpaper. He was also feeble and could hardly walk. And at this time he was snoring deeply, sound asleep in a corner.

Now, back to Mr. Murray and me; the sparkling conversation resumed: "Do you think it will rain tomorrow?" Mr. Murray asked.

"I don't know sir," I said.

"Let's look at the forecast," he said.

He withdrew a copy of the Stamford Advocate from under his jacket. Together, we bent over the newspaper to peer at the weather report. As I leaned over, I extended one of my legs. And then it happened! Suddenly, Jupey came alive.

As if propelled from a cannon, he flashed out of a snoring slumber, rocketed across the parlor, locked his front paws around my trouser leg, and started *humping like crazy!* His eyes bulged. He panted. He slobbered. The last smoldering embers of his youth glowed again!

"Ha, ha," I gasped weakly, struggling to dislodge Jupey. "Jupey wants to play!" I kicked vainly, but he clung like a leech. Let me tell you, you can't dislodge a bulldog without help!

Then, Mr. Murray, to my amazement, viewing this sordid scene, underwent a complete personality change! "Why, you son-of-a-bitch!" he roared. Still cursing a blue streak, he grabbed Jupey by his collar, gave a yank and threw him against the wall.

At this precise moment, Miss Betty Murray, my prom date, descended the staircase into the parlor in all her glory, clad in a shimmering white dress; smiling, demure, a sixteen year old goddess, in all her pristine beauty! And there *we* were in the parlor. Mr. Murray, glasses broken, red faced and still swearing. Jupey humping air in a corner of the room, and me standing there with a stain on my trousers – which I hoped and prayed, was just saliva!

Mercifully, I will draw a curtain around what happened next.

Epilogue

Betty and I did go to the Senior Prom that night. She wore my corsage over her left breast like a badge of honor. We danced the fox trot, the waltz, the Lindy and the shag. We had raspberry punch and cookies and ice cream. Then we walked the mile back down Strawberry hill to her house. And, I kissed her…for the first time; the special kiss of two innocent sixteen-year-olds; one which we would never, ever experience again.

P.S. Mr. Murray regained his composure and banished Jupey to a kennel, where he fathered six healthy, unbelievably ugly bulldog pups. Mr. Murray never spoke of Jupey again.

Moral: If a dog is gonna' hump your leg, make sure it's a Chihuahua!

JENNY

Early in the morning, throughout the day, and at day's end, you could hear her. But rarely, could you ever see her – she was that tiny. She flitted through our apple orchard from tree to tree and only when a shower of apple blossoms revealed her presence could you make out her tiny body. But it was at dusk that she shone the brightest. As the soft summer twilight moved gently into night, you could hear her song of evening and marvel at its sweet sadness.

You see, Jenny was a Wren, a New England bird measuring about 1 ½ inches long, plain brown, unadorned, and rather dull, until you heard that voice.

That summer, I built a little bird house for Jenny. She was so tiny I used a dime to measure the entry hole, cut it out, and placed a matchstick under it for a perch. I nailed it high on the trunk of our pear tree. Jenny immediately showed her appreciation. She moved in with her mate that very afternoon.

My mother, with deep affection, called her "Jenny Wren".

The Time: *August 1932*
The Place: *My home in Stamford Connecticut*
My Age: *12*
The Cast: *Jenny, Winnie, Buzz, Huma, Hattie*

It was about this time that I bought my first BB gun with my own money, earned from my paper route. It was a pump-action model with a wooden stock, on which was emblazoned a color photo of my hero, Buzz Barton, a cowboy star of that era (Roy Rogers had yet to appear on the horizon). A cardboard tube filled with little lead BBs completed the set.

At twilight, on this particular day, I was standing in the back yard with the gun cradled on my arm. Occasionally, I'd raise the gun to my shoulder and sight at some imaginary Indian. But for some reason, this time I cocked it. (Later, under questioning, I could not recall cocking it). Nevertheless, the gun was ready to fire.

I saw Jenny about 40 yards away, a crosswind was blowing and the chance of hitting *anything* in the gathering darkness was remote, if not impossible.

I pulled the trigger. There was a pop. And Jenny fell dead at the base of the pear tree.

There was a terrible silence; then a scream. It startled me. It terrified me; because the scream was *mine*. I raced to Jenny's side. I dropped to my knees, still screaming. I picked her up, but her head hung loosely. She was dead.

Then I heard another scream. It was cousin Huma, who had witnessed it all. She ran to the house. "Aunt Hattie! Aunt Hattie!" she screamed. "Winnie killed a bird with his gun!"

I raced to the stone wall, grabbed the gun by the barrel, and, sobbing hysterically, I beat the wooden stock against the rocks; again and again and again ~ and yet again, until it was in splinters, with the barrel bent and twisted like a dead snake.

I looked up. My mother was standing on the back porch drying her hands on her apron. She took one look. She said not a word, but turned and disappeared into the house.

That night, at dinner, my father, sitting at the head of the table asked amiably, "Well Winfield, what did you do today?"

I was dumbstruck. I hung my head in shame. But Huma was not dumbstruck: "You know what Winnie did today?"

At that precise moment, my mother rose from her chair, "That will be *enough* Huma!" she snapped. "*Sit down!*"

In the stunned silence that followed, she turned to me, and with deep love and forgiveness said quietly, "Winfield has suffered enough for today."

BIRDLAND

In New York City, the walk from Madison Avenue to Broadway and 52nd Street is very short, maybe ten minutes at most. But, if you take the walk that I took, it takes years to get there. I'm referring to the distance from Benton and Bowles, a giant advertising agency at 444 Madison Avenue, to Birdland, jazz Mecca of the world at 375 Broadway – light years away.

When I took that walk, with all its ramifications, I completed the journey successfully, moving back-and-forth between two totally different worlds and, considering how it all turned out for me, I escaped relatively unscathed.

Somehow, and I still don't quite know how I did this, I moved with ease, almost daily, from the uptight, Ivy League ad game, with its Brooks Brothers suits, three martini lunches, slogans, jingles, and commuter trains to Suburbia where wives and kids awaited, to the dark, smoky dives of the jazz world, epitomized by Birdland, with its murky array of zoot suits, peg pants, be-bop horn-rimmed glasses, berets, goatees, silver horns and golden saxes, spaced-out jazz cats, hipsters, hookers and users; all mesmerized, along with me, by the pied pipers of be-bop jazz:

"Dizzy" Gillespie (Trumpet) and Charlie "Yardbird" Parker (Alto Saxophone)

In a sense, I lived in one of Dante's outer rings; an observer, yes, but of greater importance; a totally absorbed, intent listener to that wonderful music I loved – jazz.

When I learned that Dizzy and Bird were booked into Birdland for a week, I made arrangements to catch the first set (9:30 pm) every night for the entire week. The logistics were simple. I told my wife I would take the last train out to Wilton, Connecticut; that I would work late at the office, and later, drop into Birdland to catch the first set. And I did just that.

Each night I would arrive at Birdland precisely at 9:15 pm, descend the long circular staircase to the tiny bandstand, bribe the attendant (by the way, a raucous midget) who would place a chair for me in the front row, right on top of the stand. I did this every night for the entire length of the gig. It became an expected, anticipated ritual.

Now, you have to understand how I looked to these people of the jazz world. Every night, this pasty-faced white guy (me) would be there, attracting attention every night for three reasons:

1. *My Entrance*: I was in uniform: charcoal grey Brooks Brothers suit, narrow brimmed fedora hat (aka Madison Avenue crash helmet), white button down collar shirt, scarlet and black Rutgers University tie and huge, thick-soled Cordovan leather wing-tipped shoes.

2. *My Conduct*: I loved the music, and I let the musicians know it.

3. *My Exit*: Promptly, at 11:00 pm I would pay my tab, rise, and flick a salute to the audience and exit up the winding staircase.

Then one night, I had just settled into my usual seat as Diz and Bird prepared to come on stage. But instead, this time, they suddenly veered off and took chairs, one on each side of me. Each took one of my ears and said: "Okay, white boy, what the fuck is goin' on?" I blanched, and told them why I was there. Then they both mounted the stand, but not before they said: "Don't go anywhere, white boy. Stay put."

And I did.

When the set was over they came back. Then, I knew I was doomed. I would never get to Wilton, Connecticut that night. And I didn't.

We went to an after-hours club deep in the heart of Harlem. I got a little drunk, but only a little, because I wanted to remember that night for the rest of my life. And I do.

Dizzy and Bird jammed with a group that included Theolonius Monk, Max Roach, Ray Brown, Lennie Tristano, Fats Navarro, John La Porta, Billy Bauer and Red Rodney – and I knew every one of them.

That evening marked a fusion with Diz and Bird, which changed my life and altered my soul…..forever.

Subsequently, my friendship with them led to my producing, on radio, on the Mutual Broadcasting Network, a series of three half-hour jazz programs featuring Dizzy and Bird with an all-star lineup of jazz musicians. It was wildly successful and generated 3,000 fan letters and postcards.

Epilogue

Now, getting back to the beginning of this story; did I say I escaped unscathed? Let's look at the facts: I am now, more than ever, at the age of 90, an unrepentant, unreconstructed jazz lover. It is first, last and always, My Grand Passion.

SPITFIRE

Spitfire was the name of a World War II British fighter plane; streamlined, dainty as hell, but packing four 50 caliber machine guns and a cannon. Spitfire was also the name of a beautiful 20-year-old British woman test pilot, also streamlined, dainty as all hell, but packing flaming red hair and a body to match.

The time: May 1944
The place: Aldermaston Air Base, England
The occasion: World War II

I was a green Second Lieutenant, training with the Paratroops, who would land behind enemy lines in Normandy, France. D-Day, June 6, 1944, was but a month away. Across the field was a factory which built Spitfire fighters. Each day I would see a Spitfire being tested or "wrung-out," 25, 000 feet up. Loops, rolls, chandelles and lazy-eights were performed, followed by a full power, straight down dive; then a pull out and a swooping dip to a gentle landing.

One morning I could not stand it any longer. I commandeered a Jeep and drove across the tarmac as the Spit taxied in and came to a stop. I wanted to meet the test pilot. The pilot cut the engine and the prop stopped whirling. I was not prepared for what happened next. The pilot slid back the canopy, pulled off the helmet and a waterfall of flaming red hair fell to her shoulders. The *he* was a *she*.

"Hello," I said. She nodded and smiled. I immediately stepped into the batter's box. "Will you join me for a drink?" She looked me up and down, sizing me up. She must have liked what she saw, because she said, "I'd be delighted."

So began a torrid love affair that took us to London and Scotland for out-of-this world weekends – and a lot more. We spent every minute, and I mean every available minute together. We went to London. We had high tea at the Hampshire House, cocktails at the Regent Palace. We kissed at every opportunity, especially during the blackouts when enemy bombers grumbled overhead.

She kidded me about our respective ranks. I was nothing but a Second Lieutenant, while she was Royal Air Force Flying Officer. She definitely out-ranked me. She would lean across the table over a martini, eyes slightly closed in that quiet but super-charged sexuality that women get when they *want* you, and she'd say: "Win, I'm giving you a direct order. Let's go to bed."

You would be surprised at the alacrity with which I responded; for she was a natural red head…all over.

We were both in another zone, where there was no war, only pure delight.

One day she said to me: "Let's fly to Scotland."

"But your Spit can't take two people."

"Oh yes it can, darling."

"How?"

"I had the armor plating behind the pilots seat removed, and a small jump seat installed."

And so it came to pass that we flew to Edinburgh, Scotland, me jammed into the jump-seat behind her, barely able to move. But I could move a little, and when I leaned over and kissed her neck, she would waggle the wings.

We stayed in a Medieval Castle in Scotland, and, after our lovemaking, we would lie in bed in the twilight listening to the skirl of the bagpipes as the castle guard changed shifts.

Then one lazy May afternoon, she took off to test a new Spitfire. I ambled across the field to wait for her. She did several loops, tight turns, spins and lazy eights; then the finale, the power dive from 25,000 feet, straight down. And down…and down…and down. At 5,000 feet she was still in a steep dive. I jumped to my feet. At 2000 feet the wings tore off. "Bail out! Bail out! Bail out!" I screamed. The Spitfire smashed into the ground and exploded. There was no parachute…..only a funeral pyre of thick black smoke.

Epilogue

I could say to you that I somehow managed to move on with my life. And, I'd be right. And, I'd be wrong. Because recently, I went to an air show of World War II aircraft at Long Beach, CA; there, high up, doing stalls, spins, chandelles and lazy-eights was a 1944 Spitfire. The Spitfire touched down daintily, taxied up to the tarmac and stopped. A hand slid the canopy back. And in my mind's eye, I saw again, amid the smoldering embers of my long-lost youth, *my* Spitfire.

DRUG STORE COWBOY

When I was in infantry combat in World War II, the following things were in plentiful supply:

1. A chance to visit interesting countries like France, Italy, Holland, Belgium and, of course, beloved Germany

2. A chance to languish on the beaches of fabulous Normandy in France or Anzio in sunny Italy, or, in the Pacific Theater, Okinawa or Iwo Jima.

3. And, of course, last but *not* least, the chance to experience all of the above and, at some point, get yourself killed in the process.

Ah yes, those indeed were the days. The possibilities were unlimited.

However….there was *one* great thing the Army offered us. The *one thing* that was available to us at *all* times – the *one thing* that kept us all in high spirits. *The one indispensable thing, available at all times….*issued with a smile. Free, just for the asking! CONDOMS!

All we had to do to obtain them was line up at the dispensary (where emaciated eunuchs called medics doled out the latex), gather in our ration and bolt out the gate, on leave to such cities as London, Paris, and Rome to sample the erotic delights each city offered, namely, women as young and eager as we were.

All of this was well and good as long as the war lasted, but when the bells of victory pealed, we found ourselves, millions of us, heading back to tiny home towns barely touched by the war…..and its sexual backwaters.

So, if we wanted to have protected sex (and we all did), we would have to, *ourselves alone,* visit the local drug store, sidle up to the elderly, bespectacled pharmacist who had known us since we were in the cradle, who knew all our family members, and, with blushing mien, ask for the forbidden fruit.

I WAS ONE OF THEM.

And so it came to pass that I found myself once more in civilian clothes, my honorable discharge button blazing from my lapel, moving toward the prescription counter of the F.C. Gross drug store in beautiful downtown Glenbrook, Connecticut, circa 1945. Gone was the protective cloak of anonymity provided by the army during the war. If I wanted to purchase condoms, I would have to do it in full view of my hometown. I was naked; an emperor without clothes, slinking up to the counter on my shameful errand.

"Hello, Winfield, glad you're back safe and sound," said Mr. Gross. "I hear you've already landed a job in New York."

"Yes, sir."

"How's your Dad and Mom?"

"Fine."

"Harold and Hazel?"

"Fine."

At this point, I felt a tap on my shoulder. It was Madame Bouvier, my high school French teacher. "Monsieur Winfield Goulden!" she cooed. "Oh, mon pauvre enfant! Mon cher, you're back safe at last," and she planted a lipstick loaded kiss on my cheek. "Comment ca va?"

"Fine," I said, blushing.

Mr. Gross leaned across the counter; "So, Winfield, what can I do for you?"

I looked at him. I looked back at Madam Bouvier, then at the line that had formed. "Just a small bottle of aspirin," I said lamely, turning red with embarrassment.

Then I slunk out the door. I had lost my first battle of civilian life.

The next day, sitting in the commuter train to New York City, I pondered my lot. The facts marched across my mind, and in grim litany they spoke:

"You are afraid to buy rubbers in a drug store in your own home town? Are you out of your mind? Coward! You're twenty-five years old, a grown man! Commanded a combat infantry company at twenty-three! Fought in France, Belgium, Holland and Germany, and you're *afraid, afraid* to buy rubbers??? Shame on me," I thought as I slumped deeper into the seat.

And then it hit me! Eureka! I've found the solution! I exalted. Ok, I thought, if I'm too embarrassed to order condoms in my home town, there's a perfect solution to this – I'll buy them in New York! In New York, where millions of people don't give a shit about anyone but themselves. New York City. Perfect anonymity! Right now, all I have to do, I thought, is take the shuttle to Times Square, hop out and into the drug store next to where I work…at 1440 Broadway.

As the train eased underground at Grand Central Station, I gathered up my stuff and bolted upstairs to the shuttle, crossed to Times Square, exited, turned right and entered that tiny corner drug store.

I had my strategy planned. When I got to the counter I'd ask the clerk for a bottle of aspirin, and in what would appear as an afterthought, for a package of Trojans. "Cool, I thought, real cool."

I approached the counter, eased into the line, and, fearlessly waited. At last it was my turn. I placed my hands on the counter:

"A bottle of aspirin, please, "I said, and a package of Trojans."

The clerk, a big, beefy, loud, red-faced, asshole, barked: "Whaaat?!"

I repeated my request again in a stage whisper. He leaned over the counter, fixed his eye on me, and with a loud, braying donkey-like laugh, shouted:

"Whatsa' matter pal….GOT A FUCKING HEADACHE?!!"

It is true that if you've experienced the worst, then it follows that nothing you experience again will ever be that bad again.

And it wasn't.

BUGLES

He stands quietly, immobilized by the numbing cold, one of his tiny mittened hands thrust deeply into his mother's fur muff. He looks up and up at the huge flag snapping in the bitter wind, hears the lanyards humming, sees the last feeble finger of setting sun on the lavender snow, feels the excitement building in his pipes.

Now comes the procession on the crunching snow, the bugle boy biting his ashen lips, flanked by the two old soldiers in Union Blue, moving at measured pace to the rattle of the snare drum.

From somewhere, comes a command. The bugle boy halts before the flagpole and snaps to attention, placing the bell of his horn smartly on his hip. The two old soldiers break ranks, shuffle forward and release the lanyards from their cleats. They move tentatively, as if disentangling themselves from a giant spider web, their trembling hands dancing on the strands.

Again, a command; the old soldiers raise seamed faces to the flag. The drummer steps one pace forward and begins a steady, measured roll. The sound is instantly snatched away. The bugler puts horn to lips and begins to blow "To the Colors." The lanyards creak as the flag is slowly lowered. The little boy raises his hand in tremulous salute. The last notes die and we are left with but the sound of the wind as the old men struggle to gather in the flag. A blast staggers them, as with halting step, they move to rejoin the formation. At the command, they all do a ragged about face and move out. The old soldiers' legs falter as they try to get in step. The little boy drops his salute and follows the formation, clinging tightly to his mother's billowing skirt.

It is December 16, 1927, I am eight years old and my mother and I are standing retreat at the old soldiers' home in Noroton, Connecticut. My uncle, Captain Arthur Carlton Bennett, is Commandant of this home. It is dark now, we are making our way to the mess hall – and my stomach is growling.

HAIL CAESAR!

To me, it sounded like a doomsday announcement. The story appeared in our home town newspaper. It said:

"Seventh grade members of the Burdick Junior High School Drama Club will present "Julius Caesar," a play by William Shakespeare, this Friday evening, April 1st at 8:00 pm in the school Assembly Hall. Admission is Free."

Why doomsday? Because somehow, some way, I was talked into appearing in this production as a Roman Soldier, not necessarily in a starring role, but as it turned out on that memorable evening, a role that, though brief, would bring me instant fame, and I would long be remembered for my performance. Years later, former classmates, friends and family would reminisce about my dramatic skills. And, they would giggle hysterically.

I still remember exactly how I got talked into this role. "Blondie" Dorflinger was the guilty party, and I was in love with "Blondie".

"Blondie" Dorflinger, the love of my life, the shining star of my existence; blond, petite, with a curving smile, ruby lips and flashing white teeth. (You know, it makes me wonder, though, even now, how in hell someone so beautiful could possibly possess a god-awful name like that – Dorflinger!!!)

"Winnie," she said firmly, "you are going to be in this play." She said this with complete conviction and there was steel in her voice when she continued: "Winnie, you better sign up…..or…," and her voice trailed off ominously: Hence, my use of the word 'doomsday'.

When rehearsals started, with Blondie's insistence, I read for every speaking part, the lead and all the supporting roles. And I failed all of them gloriously. But wait! Unbeknownst to me, Blondie, working behind the scenes, got me a gig. Finally, three things were supposed to happen:

1) I was to play a Roman soldier
2) I had one speaking line
3) My name and role would be listed in the program

Blondie was ecstatic. I was enigmatic.

As a Roman soldier, I was to wait in the wings until, on cue, I was to step on stage, raise my shield and announce: "Dispatches from Gaul," then step quietly into the back row of the on-stage ensemble.

Now my role as a Roman soldier also required me to carry a shield and brandish it. One small problem – where to get a Roman shield? Answer: Winnie would make one by hand himself in Shop class. And so it was that, in Mr. Lovell's fifth period Shop class, I made a wooden shield. It was a work of art. I put an original design on the front and nailed leather straps to the back so that I could slide my arm under and through the straps and brandish the shield.

I was ready for my moment!

The evening of "Julius Caesar" was clear and warm. The Assembly Hall was packed with the whole town because everybody had kids in Burdick Junior High. The student orchestra, complete with off-key trumpets and scraping violins, sawed with grim determination at the unrecognizable overture.

Then the play began.

There I stood, just off-stage, ready for my moment in the footlights glare. I stared out at the audience and I saw my Mom and Dad, my brother Harold, my sister Hazel, and my two Grandmothers; the whole kit and caboodle – my whole family! History was about to be made.

But "Hark!" I came to attention in a rush! It was my cue line! And, as if shot from a cannon, I leaped on stage and bellowed: "DISPATCHES FROM GAUL!"

Simultaneously, with all the strength I could muster in one gigantic swoop, I brandished the shield at arms length. Suddenly the shield broke loose from the forearm straps and, with an audible whoosh, flew all the way across the stage, practically decapitated the lead actor, slammed onto the stage with an ear-splitting 'whack' and ricocheted stage left.

I stood stupefied. Every cast member froze on the spot! But, not the audience, they burst into uncontrollable, helpless, roaring laughter. The rafters shook! Chaos reigned! Then someone, mercifully, closed the curtain.

A few minutes later, order was restored. The school Principal stepped forward and he was wonderful. He said: "Ladies and gentlemen, you should have seen that in rehearsal!" That brought down the house again. Then all was quiet. "I am sure," he said softly, "that in spite of the unexpected events of this evening, we, as adults, all owe our boys and girls up here on stage, your applause and, most importantly, your respect for their efforts tonight."

The audience echoed his remarks with cheers and thunderous applause.

Then he said: "Ladies and gentlemen, let us now continue the play."

Afterward, no one took me to task. Even my drama teacher hugged me. And in that long-lost moment in the distant 30's, I had become a folk hero.

Epilogue

There are but a handful of us left now, but when I went back East for a "Julius Caesar" reunion they remembered me. Because, when I entered the restaurant, as one, they leaped to their feet, raised their glasses high and bellowed, "DISPATCHES FROM GAUL!"

LOVE AFFAIR

The snake slowly raised its triangular head, its flirting tongue searching the pre-dawn darkness with an invisible sensory beam, its body sliding through the dew-coated grass. From time-to-time it paused, head weaving, eyes twinkling in the refracted moonlight.

The rabbit dozed in its cage, one of a group of empty hutches clustered on the outskirts of the farm adjacent to the meadow. It was a very young rabbit, white with pink eyes and an inquisitive nose. As the darkness receded and the dawn turned all things grey, the rabbit shifted slightly and sniffed sleepily at the half-eaten carrot on the floor. Then it dozed again.

The snake could not see, but even from this distance, it felt the presence of the rabbit. It raised its head high, traversing the area for a clue, and at this moment the first sun's ray lanced through the grey and illuminated the outcropping of hutches at the meadow's edge.

The same sun's ray roused the rabbit. It stretched and hopped to a corner of the cage, thrusting its muzzle through a small hole in the chicken-wire enclosure.

At that moment it saw the snake.

When the rabbit saw the snake, it leaped straight up and kept on leaping, thumping its head again and again on the roof of the cage. It was this sound that brought the snake to full alert. It paused, raising its head to maximum extension and then, it too, saw the rabbit.

For a moment, the rabbit ceased its frantic leaps and crouched, quivering, on the cage floor. Its eyes were iridescent with terror and its flanks fluctuated wildly with each breath. Then it resumed its leaps.

Again and again its sinewy legs propelled it upward with great force and it would smash against the cage ceiling, and then collapse limply to the floor.

The snake was now at the edge of the hutches, scanning each to determine which contained the rabbit. This was not a difficult task, since the rabbit was making even more noise, thrashing about as it redoubled its efforts to escape. It pushed its nose futilely against the hole in the wire, but it was too small and could not be enlarged. The rabbit's muzzle became raw and bloody in its attempts to force an escape. But, although the size of the hole would not permit the rabbit to escape, it would permit the snake to enter.

Leisurely, the snake slid towards the cage. At full extension, it was able to completely encircle the cage as it sought to get at the rabbit. At length, it found the hole in the wire. Cautiously, the snake surveyed the hole. Carefully it eased the rest of its length into a tight coil so that when it struck, the spring-like force would project it through the opening to the rabbit.

Satisfied, the snake thrust its head through the hole. There it paused, its merciless eyes focused on the rabbit, its fangs with their tiny poison ducts clearly visible. Hunter and hunted faced the moment of truth.

Strangely quiet now, the rabbit looked calmly into the snake's eyes and saw death. It was mesmerized, frozen, beyond all hope, ready for the executioner.

At that moment the snake struck.

Precisely at that moment the rabbit flashed sideways. The dripping fangs missed the rabbit and hooked into the wire mesh. Recovering, the rabbit leapt backward, putting the maximum distance between it and the snake.

The force of the snake's strike had driven it half way, but not all the way through the hole and now the girth of the snake's body at mid-length was such that it could not slip through the hole into the cage, nor could it ease itself backward outside of the cage because its fangs were entangled in the wire. It was stuck, trapped now like its prey. And so the initiative passed from one to the other. Now the hunter became the hunted.

For a long time the rabbit sat motionless. Not so the snake. While the portion of its body trapped inside the cage remained immobile, the portion of its body outside writhed and twisted in continuous convulsions.

Finally, the rabbit roused from its catatonic state. Somehow, within the clouded recesses of its brain, a message was getting through. No one will ever know why, but suddenly the rabbit leaped at the snake and sank its teeth deeply into the scaly flank. Nor did the rabbit desist. Again and again it returned until the snake's body was torn and lifeless.

It was this scene that confronted the woman when she came to get the rabbit.

Incredulously, she circled the cage, staring in disbelief. There was the lacerated body of the snake, fangs locked in the cage wire and flanks torn asunder. And there was the rabbit, muzzle smeared with blood, sitting, shuddering uncontrollably, miraculously alive.

The woman opened the cage door. The rabbit, recognizing her, moved forward. Gently, holding the rabbit in her palms, she eased it out of the cage and drew it to her breast, murmuring soft consoling words. The rabbit felt her warmth and her compassion and when she drew it closer to her body, a feeling of peace and succor filled them both and they were as one.

Still holding the rabbit, the woman left the compound and headed to another group of buildings which surrounded a small courtyard. Nestled against the woman, the rabbit could not see what was in the courtyard. Slowly the woman extended the rabbit to arms length. Softly she murmured endearments as she paused with her back to the courtyard.

Behind her, strung out on a long wire, were the pelts of freshly skinned rabbits. Directly under each pelt were their bloody entrails.

But the rabbit could see none of this, and as the woman raised the iron bar to strike, it gently nuzzled her hand, secure and safe in its love and trust.

SLUMBER PARTY

One night, I decided to stay over at my girlfriend's apartment. She and her roommate said it would be okay to sleep on the living room sofa. Now it so happens I sleep in the nude and this night was no exception. They heaped a couple of blankets on me and, shortly thereafter, I was in dreamland.

I awoke early the next morning. It was Saturday, still quiet and peaceful. I lay there with my hands locked behind my head, half asleep, half awake. There was a knock on the door. Her roommate, Annie, raced out from the bedroom in a panic. "Oh my god – it's my mother!" she whispered.

So there you have the tableau:

- Annie's mother knocking on the door
- Annie and my girlfriend casting about in near despair
- And me, the King, lying on the sofa – nude

Then, in rapid succession, one thing led to another: "Quick!" they whispered, grabbing up my clothes and dragging me, bare-assed naked, into the bedroom. "Hide!" they hissed.

"Where?" I barked.

"There!" they pointed.

And "there" was huge pile of clothing on the floor. It was positively immense.

I got the message then, loud and clear. I dove under the pile and they covered me up completely. There were skirts and blouses and dresses and god knows what else in that pile. But of far greater significance to me, there were also scores and scores of silk stockings, pairs and pairs of panties and oodles and oodles of lacey bras!

In the living room, I could hear Annie's mom chatting amiably with the girls. But I feared not, I cared not, as I sifted through the bras. I remember particularly admiring a 34D, bright scarlet one, which I viewed through an erotic haze. Never mind the panties.

Finally, I dozed off.

When the girls came to fetch me, we had a great laugh. We sat around giggling and sipping coffee, until, finally one of them said: "Uh, Win, don't you think you ought to put on some clothes now?"

LADY DAY

*The term "**Jim Crow**" requires a definition as it is germane to the subject matter of this story. From Encarta Dictionary:*
*1. **racial discrimination** the practice of discriminating against black people, especially by operating systems of public segregation*
*2. **taboo term** a highly offensive term for a black person*

***Jim Crow** (adjective) discriminating against Black people*

The first time I saw and heard Billie Holiday, I fell in love with her…. forever.

Artie Shaw, fronting his big band, was playing a one-nighter and I was in the audience, jammed up against the bandstand with other wide-eyed kids of my generation.

The band kicked off a brand new tune called "Any Old Time". I looked up and there she was; a gardenia behind her ear, gorgeous café-au-lait complexion, and a voice that I had never heard before….and will never hear again.

> "Any old time you want me,
> I'm yours for just the asking,
> Darling…."

Her eyes were gently closed and her perfect young body swayed to the muted trumpets behind her. Tiny pearls of perspiration on her forehead, reflected in the spotlight, turned her face to sparkling diamonds. I was mesmerized.

The time: *Mid-summer, 1936*
The place: *Roton Point Park Dance Casino, South Norwalk, Connecticut*
My age: *17*

At intermission, when I approached her, others were crowding in, seeking autographs, but not me. Marching, even then, to a different drummer, I waited my turn. Then;

"Miss Holiday," I said.

She looked up, surprised, for I bore no pen and paper. I sought no autograph.

"Miss Holiday," I stammered, "I love you."

She paused, and without saying a word, kissed me gently on the check.

My next and last encounter with Billie was at a tiny jazz club in Greenwich Village, New York City. A lot of water had run under the bridge since those golden days of my teens. World War II had come and gone, and it had left its mark on me. I had changed.....and so had Billie. It was shocking. Her pain was etched on her face and I could hear it in her voice....

All the pain of being black,
All the constant police harassment,
All the jail time,
All the arrests for heroin possession,
All the mistreatment,
The lost bookings, the failed recording sessions,
All the mismanagement, had taken its toll.

For *then*, there was NOBODY there for her.
There was no Martin Luther King,
There was no Rosa Parks,
There was no Medgar Evers,
There was no Bobby Seale,

There was no Malcolm X,
There was no Gil Scott-Heron.

There was only Billie…..alone…..with her hell fires of hallucination and despair.

And I could hear it all when she sang this song about the lynching of a black man:

"Southern trees bear a strange fruit
Blood on the leaves
And blood on the root

Pastoral scene of the gallant South
The bulging eyes and twisted mouth

For here is a fruit
For the crows to pluck and
The wind to suck
Here is a strange
And terrible fruit"

Billie paid a terrible price. She became a heroin addict.
But – it was not heroin that killed Billie……
It was Jim Crow.

A GATHERING OF EAGLES

In the spring of 1937, at a specially convened Court of Honor in Stamford, Connecticut, my father pinned on my chest the Boy Scouts of America's highest award – the Eagle Scout badge. Little did I know that this moment would set in motion an unbelievable sequence of events which would propel me, in four short months into a face-to-face meeting with the President of the United States.

There was to be, in Washington D.C., in the summer of that year, an International Boy Scout Jamboree, a gathering of Boy Scouts from the four corners of the earth.

We had an encampment at the base of the Washington Monument, and we met fellow Boy Scouts from every country in the world. We would visit each others encampment, swapping souvenirs with boys from France, England, Spain, India, and many, many other countries. In the sweltering heat of that long ago summer, we joined hands with our Scout brothers in peace and harmony.

But the German contingent was different – very different. They were not permitted to fraternize individually with Scouts from other countries. Instead, they marched everywhere in formation under the watchful eye of their leaders. With their swastika arm bands, they were all tall, all blond, and all very aloof. (I did not know it then, but seven years later, I would meet them again in their Nazi SS Units on the beaches of Normandy, France, under very different circumstances).

Then one day, our troop Scoutmaster called us all together and announced, to our joyous surprise, that our scout troop had been selected to send one Eagle Scout to represent the New England states in a guard-of-honor for President Franklin Delano Roosevelt at the 1937 Major League Baseball All-Star game in Griffith Stadium in D.C.

I was that Eagle Scout.

And when the great day dawned, we Eagle Scouts, resplendent in our merit badge sashes, formed a guard-of-honor for the President as he threw out the first ball. The President shook hands and chatted with each of us, but to this day, I cannot remember what he said to me, because, standing right beside me on the playing field was my idol, Joe DiMaggio, only in his second year in the major leagues.

We marched out to center field. We raised the flag. Then we stood at attention and held the Boy Scout Salute as the band played the Star Spangled Banner. It was some moment.

Epilogue

I am an old man now, comfortable with my fond memories, but, in the end, what I remember most vividly of all is this:

When my father, a most taciturn man, pinned the Eagle Scout badge on my chest so long ago, he looked deeply into me, and I saw then, as I see now, the tears in his eyes as he whispered, "God bless you son."

GENESIS

For four hours, we have been driving across the desert floor. The merciless sun sets the steering wheel ablaze, and I hold it gingerly. We are zombies, our bones dried and caked with fatigue, prisoners of whirling dust devils in the desert's bleak, impersonal hell. Far, far on the horizon, we see the mountains, made iridescent by the shimmering waves of heat rising from the sticky pungency of the asphalt ribbon upon which we are astride. A procession of tumble-weeds comes bounding toward us. Too tired to swerve, I let each one bounce off the front bumper and deposit its skeletal remains on the windshield. She offers me a sip of water from a plastic bottle, but when I press it to my cracked lips, the water is lukewarm and brackish. Suddenly, the sky directly ahead darkens, and in a finger snap, the sun is gone and darkness surrounds us.

It is a sandstorm.

Despite the darkness, the heat does not abate. It gets hotter, and what little visibility there is diminishes swiftly as the wall of sand rapidly approaches us. And then it slams into us, and even though I have already parked by the side of the road in anticipation of this, the storm hits full force with the hissing of a thousand snakes. The car rocks wildly. Needle points of sand sift through every crack, every crevice, every tiny opening throughout the entire car. I have kept the engine running deliberately, but I know that this precaution will be but momentary, unless the storm quickly abates. Otherwise, in a matter of minutes, the sand will have infected the engine and it will die a twisted, strangling death.

And then suddenly, it is gone.

Where before the storm was monstrous, now it is but scattered remnants of itself as it dissipates into hundreds of tiny dust devils, each dying a slow death into nothingness, much like the dissolving witch of Oz. Then wondrously, sky, horizon and desert rearrange themselves in perfect order and I look up and the mountains are close, very close upon us. It is as if they have moved forward with a momentum of their own.

We look at each other. We smile. And a great peace descends upon us.

The climb is gentle and unhurried as we glide gradually upward, ever upward into the lush foothills at the mountain's base. The sun is bright, but it is a clean, benevolent sun, and its benign rays are soft, warm and caressing.

Then, it starts to rain, but there is no rush of water, no torrent, but instead a soft, cleansing shower that slides gently down the windshield. The sun's gleaming rays, impacting the rain, turn earth and sky into glittering diamonds.

We look at each other. I bring the car to a stop. We jump out, quickly shedding our clothing. We look at each other again. And now, our bodies are also glittering diamonds. I open my arms, and she moves into them. We kiss and the diamonds are everywhere…on our tongues, and throughout our bodies as we dance the dance

    – of love
    – and life
    – and hope

52ND STREET

There were three of us
All World War II combat veterans
All had been wounded
And all were jazz lovers

World War II was over at last
We were in our early twenties
And suddenly
We were bound together and cast – like dice
Smack dab into the middle of the New York jazz scene
Fifty Second Street
One city block packed with every kind of jazz
Imaginable

And from the get-go, we all took to Fifty Second Street
Like a duck takes to water

For we were all jazz fans
With leanings toward the likes of Duke Ellington, Stan Kenton,
Count Basie, Artie Shaw, Woody Herman, Gene Krupa and Benny
Goodman
But what we did not know was
That when we hit the Big Apple, in addition to our traditional
favorites
We were about to be propelled – naked as a jay bird

Deeply into the Bebop revolution
That was about to alter the face of jazz
Forever

For while we might have originally
Been regarded as traditional jazz lovers
That would be wrong
Because we were young and susceptible
Our eyes were wide open to innovation
And so were our ears

Having each been in the military for five years
By force of habit
We set up a base camp
We rented a huge artist's loft
Deep in the heart of that Bohemian paradise
Greenwich Village

We stocked that loft
With booze and pot
And also with
Hot and cold running chicks
And thus
We drank often
And deeply
Of life

By the way - speaking of pot
We were all of the booze generation
Except
Once again
We were young
And, after all that World War II shit
We would try anything
We found that sex and pot mixed beautifully together
Producing an erotic haze
Through which we wandered in total abandon

We descended on 52nd Street
Like a plague of locusts
We hit every club, bar and bistro
Where jazz was being played
Clubs like Jimmy Ryan's, The Famous Door, Café Society,
The Onyx, Billie's Place, Wynn's Place and O'Dell's
Every night

And a procession of jazz heroes paraded through our
Psyches – Dizzy Gillespie, Charlie Parker, Max Roach,
Ray Brown, Charlie Ventura, Lester Young, Coleman Hawkins,
Juan Tizol, Theolonius Monk – all blowing their
Collective asses off
Every night

Now – aside from all this esoteric shit
There were practicalities to be faced:
1. What were the names of the clubs on 52nd Street?
2. How many sets were played nightly at each club and at what time?

This would involve close scrutiny
So that we could, for example, at:
9:00 pm – Catch Theolonius Monk's first set
10:00 pm – Catch the Duke Ellington band
11:00 pm – Catch Billie Holiday
Midnight – Catch Dizzy Gillespie and Charlie Parker

And guess what?
I was the one
Anointed by my two buddies
To plot a zigzag course
Up and down 52nd Street
To catch all the combos
Until closing time
Which was 4:00 am

And so it was
That I became
The gig navigator
Guiding my charges
Literally
Through a labyrinth of jazz

And
Every jazz joint
Had a uniformed doorman at curbside on the street
He, and he alone,
Knew the gig schedule
Of the musicians and vocalists
Not only at his club
But all the others as well
And if you plied him
With a sip from your flask
And a freshly rolled joint
He would tell you
That Billie Holiday
Had just finished her set at his club
And was
Even as he spoke
Across the street at the Famous Door
Sitting in
With the Duke Ellington band

Well, it was one hell of an experience
I'll tell you
One hell of a run
Three horny, hungry, happy young Turks
Roaming
And owning
52nd Street

Two months later
Our golden journey

Came to an end
Our money had run out

In the beginning
We had pooled all of our Army mustering-out pay
And now it was gone
And we all knew
That when the money was gone
We would be gone too

We also made a solemn agreement
That when we split up
We would never seek out each other again
We did not exchange addresses
We did not exchange phone numbers
We just split
For good

Now
I have no idea where my buddies are
Or whether they're alive or dead
It doesn't matter
Because
At that time
Each of us knew
With a wisdom beyond our years
That any future reunion
Would never
Ever
Duplicate
That brief, joyous flash of our youth

BABYFACE

Ahead, I could see a sliver of silver on the horizon. "There's the Rhine River," I thought.

I eased my glider higher above the tow plane to get a better look at the formation. It was the Rhine alright. I could see airborne units of the first wave already dropping on our objective, the East bank of the Rhine River, deep inside Germany.

It was March 25, 1945.

Parachutes were blooming, gliders were winging over and down. I could see the serial numbers chalked to their fuselages as they glided delicately into the battle below. As I watched, one glider released its tow line, climbing straight up until, at the apex of its stall, it broke apart, disgorging a jeep, ammo and men in a long looping cluster until they plummeted out of my sight.

A funereal pall of sooty smoke shrouded the landing zones, obscuring the carnage that was taking place below. The fields below were already a charnel house that would, before the end of this day, gobble up more glider pilots in this one operation than in any other airborne operation in World War II. The fields were already littered with collapsed chutes and crashed gliders, and, looking closely, I could see American bodies everywhere; paratroopers with their chutes fouled in trees, dangling in the rag doll attitude of violent death.

A series of sharp, ripping pops got my attention in a hurry as a Kraut anti-aircraft battery opened up on us. Bullets tore through the flimsy canvas fuselage. I heard the all too familiar 'thunk' of incoming 20 millimeter shells. The control wheel vibrated furiously as we took hits in the elevators and ailerons; just about the worst place on the glider to take a hit; next to the fuselage that housed the hapless infantrymen.

The glider infantrymen sank deeper into their own bodies, trying to make themselves smaller as the bullets sought them out. A ricochet hit the metal fuselage frame with an evil whine, and it was then that I heard the strange mewling sounds behind me, the sounds of the men back there as they froze, anuses tightening in terror.

Soon it would be our turn to land as the sky train crawled forward.

"Biggest ever," trumpeted the strutting General, Commanding Officer of the First Allied Airborne Army, to the press, "one continuous train of tow planes and gliders, stretching from Paris to the Rhine. Gentlemen, this is Vertical Envelopment!"

I glanced at the Plexiglas bubble on top of the tow plane's fuselage, watching for the green light that would be my signal to release the towrope and get the hell down on the ground, fast. My left hand gripped the control wheel; my right was on the tow rope release lever, ready to cut loose.

Thirteen men in my glider had thirty seconds left to live.

The green light flared. I hit the release lever and we started down. The ceaseless roar of being towed at 120 miles an hour softened to a gentle whoosh as we decelerated to 60 miles an hour.

But one German machine gun stayed with us all the way down. Bullets and shrapnel were tearing us up. I heard screams from behind me. I did not look back. I knew what they were and what caused them. I had heard them before.

My co-pilot turned to shout something just as he got it in the face. One second he was shouting, and then his face disintegrated. He lurched sideways and what was left of his head snuggled into my lap and in that split second we hit the ground, sliding sideways. I heard more screams from within the fuselage as the machine gun continued to track us. We spun around three times. Clouds of dirt and dust enveloped the cockpit. Our nose dug in. We were down.

I unbuckled my seat belt, grabbed my Tommy-gun and dove out the side window of the cockpit just as the glider took a direct hit from a German mortar.

The glider disintegrated, hurling bodies, some still screaming, everywhere. And at that precise moment, I took one in the knee. The pain was exquisite, beyond feeling, beyond comprehension. Dimly, I realized that I had lost all my men except one, and he was a civilian Associated Press photographer who volunteered, repeat, volunteered for this glider mission.

I realized that we had to get off the field and get to that ditch, which was about 50 yards away. We were in the open field in the beaten zone of that machine gun. We had to get to that son-of-a-bitch. We just had to.

The machine gun was at the juncture of two ditches bordering the field. I could see the flash of its muzzle blast. I kept crawling, dragging my leg along. I was losing blood rapidly and I was getting giddy. The air crackled inches above my head and I heard the *whump! whump!* of German mortars as the shells walked back and forth in the midst of our wounded, dead, and dying.

I heard a voice yelling over and over again, "That's enough! That's enough!" and suddenly I realized that the voice was my own.

And then I saw Art. Art, my buddy, a cab driver from Menomonee, Michigan, tall lanky, homely as a hedge fence, and fearless.

"Jesus," he panted, looking at my kneecap which was dangling by a shred of tissue. I started to look down but he grabbed me. "Don't look at it!" he yelled, "Don't look at it!" He twisted his head, scanning the field. "Medic! Medic! Where's a fucking Medic?"

"Art, you got grenades?

"Yeah, bagful!"

"Ya' spot him?"

"Yeah, corner ditch!"

"We gotta rush him!"

"We'll never make it, neither of us!"

Art raised his head slightly, "I think I can get him from here!" And, at this point we lucked out. The Kraut gunner suddenly shifted his fire upward to rake the waves of gliders still floating in.

Art stood up and lobbed a grenade. At the same time, lying on my side, I lobbed in two grenades. We pressed ourselves into the earth. We heard the *whamp! whamp! whamp!* Art catapulted up and charged the ditch, firing as he ran. Simultaneously, I opened up with the Tommy-gun, giving him covering fire.

The machine gun stopped suddenly. It was absolutely still. I dragged myself the remaining distance to the gun. Art was already there, standing over the gun. There was a body draped over the barrel.

Art placed his boot on the dead German's chest and gave a shove. And what a strange sight; the body was badly mutilated, but the face was intact. And it was the face of an angel. It was the face of a child.

"Jesus," Art said softly, "Look at this, no uniform, just a fucking kid."

"Yeah," I said, surveying the carnage out on the fields, "Just a fucking kid."

LADY IN WAITING

Though it was already dawn, she was still bathed in icy grey and gave off no warmth. Fog shrouded her fuselage and her wingtips were barely visible.

He peered into the cockpit. The meager cluster of instruments, each with its coat of luminous paint, glowed dully in the gloom and moisture dripped from their faces. He fished around inside, came up with a rag and wiped the tiny windshield. He removed the parachute and harness dangling from his shoulder. Hoisting it over the cockpit lip, he mashed it into the bucket seat. He looked at the dried stalks and patches of hardened grain that were clustered like buckshot on what passed for a runway.

The windsock hung limp and wrinkled, like an old man's penis. Somewhere, out in this Kansas back land, a rooster crowed.

Placing his foot in the fuselage stirrup, he vaulted into the cockpit, settling in with a whoosh. He adjusted the safety belt, buttoned his wind breaker, brought a long white scarf to his forehead and wiped his goggles.

The mechanic stood sleepily in front of the prop. "Off and closed," he growled, and began to turn the prop. At first he turned it with ease, but gradually his efforts became more labored as the engine compression began to build. Finally he stopped. They exchanged shouts: "Contact!"

The mechanic cocked his leg and pulled down hard on the prop. For an instant, nothing happened. Then there was a gurgle, a sharp bang, and smoke belched from the exhaust stacks. Inside the cockpit, he advanced the throttle with one hand and with the other worked the wobble pump. "Come on baby," he whispered, "come on."

The wind-milling prop became a blur as the engine caught and he felt her shake into life. He throttled back to a lower RPM, but even at idle she quivered against the wheel chocks like a bronco in the chute. He waved to the mechanic, pulled the goggles onto the bridge of his nose and, wings wagging crazily, waddled out to the runway.

He flipped on the wing lights, but their glow was muted by the heavy fog. A chill settled into the cockpit and as he fish-tailed from side to side along the runway, he began to reflect. "Was this just a ground fog? Was it only a few hundred feet thick? Would he be able to climb up through it to the clear and open sky on top? Or was it several thousand feet thick?"

He tossed aside this sinister possibility. After all, he was twenty years old. He had 30 hours solo time. He feared nothing and he knew everything. He was committed. "We go," he thought.

At the far end of the field he turned onto the runway and stopped, ran up the engine, scrunched down in the seat and settled in for the takeoff run. He released the brakes, gave her full throttle and they were on their way. He felt vibrations in his feet as the wheels trundled over the uneven ground. She gathered speed, the vibration ceased, and they were airborne.

Instantly, he was enveloped in darkness. The fog was so thick that he could no longer see his wingtip lights. His world ended six inches in front of the windshield.

He was a prisoner.

He thrust his head forward to take in the flight instruments, his eyes flitting from dial to dial, constantly scanning. Minutes passed. He was at 1500 feet and still in the stuff. Rivulets of moisture crawled across the windshield in unending succession, twisting into strange configurations in the prop blast. Fog was saturating his thin windbreaker and he constantly wiped his goggles. The moisture was even collecting on his palms. He glanced down and realized the truth. It was not fog. It was sweat.

Suddenly, he burst through the overcast into blazing sunlight. The rays touched the millions of droplets on the wings, turning them into sparkling diamonds and she blinked with a thousand lights. Then, in an instant they were gone, evaporated by the slipstream.

He eased the throttle back to cruising speed, heaved a deep sigh and looked around. Everywhere there were clouds, but more important to him, they were already beginning to break up under the sun's warm rays. Soon there would be holes in the overcast and they would be his avenues back to earth and safety.

He glanced off to the right. The roiling clouds were thinning and unfolding into fantastic shapes. Off the wing, he saw a group of horses, their riders in Roman tunics with helmets and breastplates of burnished gold. He twisted and looked down. Rising slowly, a thousand feet below, an old man with a beard stretched his hands in supplication, an impish parrot perched on his shoulder. He eased the throttle forward and began to climb to the sun. The altimeter revolved steadily, ticking off the altitude like a metronome, and he thought, "How high can she go? What's her absolute ceiling?"

He decided to find out. He began a series of wide sweeping climbing turns. Each revolution brought him to a higher altitude. He reached 10,000 feet and continued to climb. At 12,000 feet he began to feel strange. The air was rapidly thinning and he remembered that above 10,000 feet one should be on oxygen. The rate of climb began to slow. The engine was laboring and the propeller no longer bit off huge chunks of air. His swift and thrilling ascent had slowed to a painful crawl. His breath became clearly visible with each exhalation, and the cold settled heavily on him. He watched the altimeter crawl agonizingly through 14,000, then 14,500. He decided to level off at 15,000, but in the next instant that decision was taken away from him. Aerodynamics and the laws of physics had taken over.

She was wallowing. A strange deadness set in. He glanced at the airspeed. It was dropping. He need not have looked. He could feel the fatigue throughout the entire airframe. The engine was turning at full power, but they remained in a climbing attitude, hanging by the prop, motionless and spent. She could go absolutely no further. She was going to stall.

He flashed a last glance at the altimeter. The controls went slack. Then she gave up. The wings wobbled and lost their lift. She dropped heavily. He popped the stick forward to get the nose down and pick up airspeed, but in the thin air he had to be patient. She was running away from him. Now, he had to wait for her, wait till they dropped to heavier air where once again he could gain complete control.

She rolled over on a wing and whipped into a tight spin. He looked over the nose straight down at the revolving checkerboard below. He throttled back to lessen the strain on her, the G's of the turns, even in this biplane, began to multiply inside the cockpit and he was pressed tightly into the seat.

He let her go a little longer. He was beginning to be disoriented and found difficulty in reading the altitude. He felt her pulsations and knew that the time had come to take her back. Inside of him, a voice said "Now." He kicked opposite rudder, shoved the stick forward and waited. She fought him for a moment and then she surrendered and they came out of it in a long sweeping, graceful, controlled dive. He eased the stick back and they resumed level flight.

She was his once again.

He looked below and began a series of shallow turns to get his bearings, searching for some familiar landmark. Then he spotted the railroad track and he was reconnected, in control, knowing exactly where he was. He relaxed. Now he decided to reward both of them. He pulled the stick back and rose up in a graceful Chandelle, a beautiful name for a beautiful maneuver; a 180 degree climbing turn, invented, or stumbled on, by Auguste Chandelle, a World War I French Ace.

He spotted a herd of cumulus clouds and plunged joyfully into their depths. The cockpit flashed on and off as he flitted from cloud to sunlight to cloud. Their cool moisture bathed his face and he laughed aloud. He coordinated stick and rudder in a slow roll until he was upside down. He looked up at the Kansas checkerboard, a mosaic in browns and greens with blond wheat fields placed like postage stamps in their midst. He looked down and saw nothing but brilliant blue. The sun glinted on his goggles. He was in euphoria.

Now he was over the field. He throttled back to idle and put her into a long slanting glide. She was alive with sounds and scents; her wires sang, taut and vibrant; he smelled her engine oil, sharp and pungent, and he heard the whapping of her idling prop. Far off the wing, he spotted a flock of geese, holding formation in a pulsing V.

He entered traffic, turned for the final approach and he felt the hot breath of Kansas summer. He eased the stick backward and forward, ever so slightly, feeling for the ground as they came in over the fence. Then they were down, the wheels grumbling and the tail sinking as the weight shifted from the wings to the landing gear. At the end of the landing roll, he taxied back to the hanger. A morning breeze had come up and the windsock was now erect.

Then he saw her standing on the tarmac. She was his girl. She was eighteen and she was waiting for him. The sun at her back touched her body, revealed her lovely breasts, softly shading her secret places.

Now he stood before her. She pulled back, and with a mock pout said, "You forgot about me!"

He turned back and looked long at the plane. "No" he thought, "you forgot about her."

BEWARE OF FOREIGN ENTANGLEMENTS

If I had known what was going to happen to me on that fateful day, I would never have boarded that damned bus.

The place:	*Stamford, Connecticut – population: 35,000*
The year:	*1935*
The weather:	*Snowing*
The temperature:	*28 degrees Fahrenheit and dropping*
The time:	*5 pm*
My age:	*16 years*

I dropped in my token, unbuttoned my trench coat and worked my way down the aisle. The bus lurched into gear and I squeezed into the only seat available next to a portly woman whose girth was such that she was already encroaching on my space. She was a hennaed red-head with a face mask of raging rouge and fiery lipstick – a kewpie doll.

She wore a huge, oversized imitation fox fur coat and she clutched a large bag of groceries to her ample bosom. "Pardon me, ma'am," I said, shoe-horning my body into the tight space. She turned, her grocery bag crackling, and stared blankly at me. We were so tightly pressed that any slight move on my part immediately provoked another crackling stare from her.

Uncomfortable and ill-at-ease, I sighed in resignation and wearily extended my legs into the aisle.

The bus grumbled on, making its stops, my eyes grew heavy, and I almost dozed. Suddenly, I became aware that a young girl facing me from across the aisle seemed to be staring at me. A second later I caught her. She was staring at me for sure, with an enigmatic smile on her lovely face – and she was staring directly at my loins.

I glanced down and recoiled in panic. My god! My fly was unzipped and wide open! In terror, I pressed myself against my portly seat companion to hide my open fly. Frantically, I started to zip up, but it stuck half way. It would not go further. I tugged. I squirmed to zip it, but it was jammed solid.

I had zipped it into her imitation fox fur coat! And as I pressed tightly against her, she turned and looked directly at me again. But this time, no blank stare. She glared at me with outright suspicion! So, there I was – stuck. Every time she moved, I moved with her. We were Siamese twins, joined at the hip! "My god," I thought, as the sweat broke out. "What can I do?"

In desperation, I slid my hand into my pants pocket. (Now, as an aside, let me say that most boys, in those days carried a tiny pocket knife; not a switchblade, mind you; a tiny pocket knife). Swiftly, I extracted the knife, opened it and turned toward the woman. Then I really panicked. She was getting up, bag crackling. In one last desperate move, I seized her coat as she was rising and, with one deft movement, I sliced off the tip of the fur.

She rose and waddled down the aisle and got off at her stop. Dazed, sweating like a pig, hands trembling, I buttoned my coat, rose, staggered down the aisle and hung onto a strap, panting as the doors opened for me.

The wintry blast revived me. It was now snowing heavily and I had a half mile yet to trudge. Looping my scarf around my neck, I forged on, finally arriving at my home. I mounted the porch steps, stamped off the snow and opened the front door. Inside it was pitch dark. I fumbled for the light switch, but suddenly, all the lights in the front room blazed.

"SURPRISE!! HAPPY BIRTHDAY!!" came a shout of voices.

There stood my family, my mother and father, sister, brother, my grandmothers, the whole family! I shucked off my trench coat. And…. the happy shout died in their throats and became a collective gasp of horror!

I looked down. I had completely forgotten. For there, zipped securely into my fly, bobbing up and down obscenely like a furry phallus, was a huge tuft of imitation fox fur.

BLOOD BROTHERS

The snow was heavy, wet and knee deep
It clung to me like glue
My eyebrows were frosted
As I stumbled across the village square
And, Tommy-gun on full automatic,
Approached the ruined church

The Time: World War II
The Date: December 25, 1944, Christmas Day
The Place: The village of Bastogne, Belgium
The Circumstance: Desperate. The German Army had launched its last and greatest attack of World War II, deep in the Ardennes Forest. It was sudden, unanticipated by the Allies, and wildly successful. American and British troops were totally surprised and overrun by the Germans, who penetrated 50 miles deep into Allied territory.

The 101st Airborne Division, to which I had been assigned, had been rushed to the front lines to meet the attack head on and stop the Germans from advancing any further, or, as our Commanding General said, "Not one more fucking inch!"

A long, bloody battle took place at this tiny Belgian village. Although we stopped the Germans, the price of war was paid in full. In all, 30,000 casualties were sustained. We had been in combat for two months and we were physically and emotionally drained, purged of all feeling, even fear of death; zombies on both sides, stalking each other in the dead

of winter. Frostbite prevailed – fingers, hands, arms and legs had to be
amputated.

It was an icy hell
We were devoid of hope
The only reality was fatigue
Bone-aching, endless fatigue
Always, the fatigue

And so it was that I slogged cautiously
Across the village square
Tommy-gun on full automatic
And approached the ruined church
I kicked open the door
Peering into the gloom
The roof had collapsed onto the altar
The place was a shambles
And then, I saw them

There sprawled before the altar
Were two soldiers
One dead American
One dead German

They must have surprised each other at the same time
They must have fired at the same time
Simultaneously killing each other
For, while their torsos were torn asunder
Their faces remained calm and peaceful
Saint like
Each had fallen,
Each, in some crazy, last moment
Had fallen into the other's arms
Their individual pools of blood were now intermingled
And they were as one
The American could not have been more than eighteen
He had red-orange hair

Freckles and a turned-up nose
The German was about the same age
Handsome, with blue eyes, light complexion
With long flaxen hair under his helmet

I looked down at them
And I remember thinking then
Even as I am thinking now, over a half-century later

What a strange place
For young boys
To be killing each other

CAFÉ DE LA PAIX

There is a café in Paris located in the heart of the city on the Champs Elysee. It is called the Café de la Paix, and it is said that if one sits at an outside table long enough, one will certainly meet someone he knows.

The Time:	*August 25, 1944 - World War II*
The Place:	*Paris, France, the Champs Elysee*
The Occasion:	*The liberation of this beautiful city of light from the Germans*
On Stage:	*Me, sitting astride a Sherman tank, my Tommy-gun in hand; a crew-cut, twenty-three year-old blond kid from Stamford, Connecticut, leading a column of tanks down this famous boulevard – into history.*

I stood up. Everywhere, *everywhere* there were thousands of cheering, screaming people, ALL joyously chanting, "Vive les Americains!"

And the girls, lovely, gorgeous, curvaceous (any cliché' you want), with their perky breasts and short skirts, pelting us with flowers, handing up glasses of wine, and an occasional bra or pair of panties, climbing aboard and showering us with kisses.

It was pure, unadulterated, divine insanity!

We halted in front of the Café de la Paix. A gaggle of waiters in their tuxedo tops and long white aprons raced to the tank, passing up bottles of champagne and cognac.

I looked down, and then I saw her long flowing waterfall of jet black hair framing her face. I reached down; she reached up; I drew her aboard. We kissed, softly, warmly, our tongues entwined.

"Get these fucking girls offa' here!" barked the tank commander. And, with great reluctance, I lowered her gently. But not before she pressed a card in my hand. It read:

Mlle Yvette Tavian
Assistante
Ministerie de Colonies
14 Rue Pontissant
Paris, France NO 321-2105

So began our romance.

Every chance I could get, whenever I got back from the front lines, I would race to her arms. We would meet all over Paris; sip Chartreuse at a tiny table in the Bois de Boulogne, kiss deeply in front of the Venus de Milo in the Louvre, kneel respectfully at the alter of the Cathedral de Notre Dame, holding hands under the prayer book.

Her brother was a prisoner of war in Germany. His clothes fit me perfectly, so we moved about the city like civilians, with me in her brothers dark blue Sunday suit (I still wore my dog tags under the shirt).

When I was wounded she somehow found the hospital I was in and pulled strings to visit me. We were six patients to a ward, and when she arrived, the other five guys (after low whistles of admiration, approval and pure lust) all left the room, but not before placing a screen around my bed for privacy.

When the war in Europe ended, this affair ended. Or did it?

I was going back to the U.S. on a hospital ship and when the order came through I saw her once more.

"When I get to America, I'll send for you," I lied.

"I'll be waiting," she lied.

And that was it. Or was it?

Forty-six years later, in 1990, I went back to Paris. I sought out the Café de la Paix, I sat sipping an aperitif with my young, beautiful new wife. We sat at an outdoor table. I looked around, remembering. Every young girl looked like Yvette. There were Yvettes everywhere. "Could it be?" I thought, "Could it be?"

"You won't find her," my wife said.

AVENUE OF THE STARS

I was forty-nine years old, back in 1968, when the Hippies first burst on the scene and, although I was not of their generation, I felt a kinship with these kids of "the movement", as it was called at that time. For one thing, believe it or not, I had ideals myself, which had yet to be sacrificed on the corporate altar on which I toiled. You might even say that beneath that Edwardian suit and flowered tie, there beat the heart of a bleeding liberal.

I would watch these youngsters gather all over Los Angeles, commandeering any plot of green, lounging together, smoking pot, hanging out, flashing the Peace Sign and waving anti-Vietnam war banners. That's what endeared them to me the most – they hated the Vietnam War. And I hated the Vietnam war too, with its brutality, maimed bodies, Agent Orange, mass murder on both sides; an endless, writhing venomous snake that could not be killed, even if you cut off its head.

I would look down from my smug, Executive Vice President corner office in a Century City high rise and see them massing for a demonstration on Avenue of the stars and I felt a deep guilt. I feel it now again when I see, in my mind's eye, that pitifully tiny Vietnamese girl, covered with napalm, her skin in tatters, running, running naked toward the camera, clothes burned off her back, looking at me and silently screaming, "Why?"

Then one night I was working late in my office. The Hippies were gathered below. I went to the window and looked down. I stood there for awhile. Then I opened the bottom drawer of my desk and took a belt of Jack Daniels, took the elevator down and marched out onto Avenue of the Stars where the Hippies were standing.

"Where the hell do you think you're goin'?" a police officer barked.

"I just want to talk to these people," I said.

"Are you out of your fuckin' mind? What are you, a nigger lover?"

This brush with the law attracted the attention of several Hippies.

"Whatta' we got going here?" one jeered.

"Look at that tie!"

"Goddamned Nixon lover!"

"Asshole!"

"Look at him! Look at that uniform!"

"Honky bastard!"

Then I lost it. I found a bullhorn lying on the ground. I grabbed it, snapped it on, "So I'm wearing a uniform, right?" I shouted. "Suit, tie, right?"

"Right!"

"Right!"

"And what the fuck do you think you're wearing, huh? Long hair, granny glasses, buckskin fringed jackets, big belt buckles, moccasins! You all look alike, covered in shit," I raved. My disappointment at being rejected roiled up from my gut, sour in my mouth. "You make me wanna puke," I snarled.

The crowd, now very large, jeered "fuck you, you prick – double fuck you!"

"You honky piece of shit!"

"Whitey pig!"

Then one of the cops yanked the bullhorn away and grabbed me in a choke hold. "Get the hell outta" here," he yelled, "or I'll book you for inciting a riot!" He released his hold, and with a kick, sent me sprawling.

The Hippies cheered. Slowly I gathered myself up and walked painfully back into the building, punched the elevator button, and walked back into my office.

I stood at the window for a long, long time, staring into the night. And, once again, I saw that pitifully tiny Vietnamese child, covered with napalm, her skin in tatters, clothes burned off her body, running, running out of the darkness and silently screaming, "Why?" "Why?" "Why?"

HEAT

His arm snakes around her lovely waist
And he nuzzles her cheek
Inhaling her fragrance
Feeling her heat

A tiny drop of sweat
Glistens on the tip of his nose
And suddenly
It drops between her breasts
And she giggles in delight

The muted trumpet
Gives off a sensual buzz
And his ears
Sing with the decibels

She presses her body to his
And he feels a stirring
As does she
And then they undulate

In the center of the dance floor
Kissing passionately
Oblivious to all

And he knows
That there will be
Many other times
And places
But, never again, quite like this

For they are both
In the bloom of their youth
Perfectly frozen
In space and time

AIR MAIL

The mechanic advanced the throttle. Oil spray wreathed the open cylinder heads, was flung headlong over the fuselage and flashed past the massive dorsal fin tail surface. The De Havilland pulsed with life, poised on tiptoe, struggling to rise from the chocks as he fed the coal to it, and then lapsed into a shudder when he throttled back.

I was ten years old and standing at a point in time, a marker in my life that had been designated for me. I was standing on the tarmac of Hadley Field, it was 1930, in Plainfield, New Jersey, and I was in love; in love with aviation, and more specifically, in love with air mail pilots. These youthful heroes of my childhood, with their Army-style brush haircuts, their fur-lined boots and flying suits, their weathered leather helmets and huge moon-like goggles, nightly took the mail out of Hadley Field to Cleveland, navigating their De Havilland bi-planes over the Allegheny Mountains, relying on luck and a line of primitive beacons lodged on evil saw-toothed ridges to guide them to the general vicinity of that city.

My first contact with the old air mail came when my brother brought me to the home of Wesley Smith. Wes stood six-feet-four and hit the marker at a solid 225 lbs. His hair was blue-black and he wore a thick, bristly moustache to compliment what was on top. He had the word "Pilot" emblazoned on his forehead, or so it seemed to me.

"So you're Winnie!" he rasped. "Well, contact!" And he swept me up over his head, turned me upside down for an instant and then grounded me safely at his feet. "There! You've just soloed. How'dja like that?"

He need not have asked. I was enthralled, and from that moment on I was also in love with Wesley Smith. It was a strange and lasting relationship; strange because of the difference in our ages, yet lasting because of our mutual love for aviation; he as a performer and I as a favored Page.

I sit here now and thread the projector of my memory and re-run the film once again. It is December, 1930, the temperature holds at 30 degrees, and I am with my brother at Wes' home in New Brunswick, New Jersey once more. We are picking Wes up and driving him to Hadley Field. He has drawn the Cleveland night run. We struggle into my brothers' Nash and the ride from New Brunswick to Plainfield is less than comfortable until Wes murmurs, "Shit!" under his breath and hoists me to his lap. I look up at him and I am directly under the classic overhang of his moustache and I can hear the sonics of his chest cavity as he booms his conversation to my brother at the wheel.

Hadley lies out there in the black, a few feeble smudgy flares outlining its boundaries. There isn't much here for one to see in daytime; a few terrified tin hangers crouched in a corner of a rolling meadow, a couple of cannibalized fuselages. But at night there is only a sickly beacon which points a tremulous finger into the darkness as it rotates the full 360.

We pull up in front of one of the sliding panels. Wes jumps out and pounds on the tin sheathing. In the winter stillness the noise is shattering.

"Axel!" he shouts, "Come on! Come on!" Slowly the doors slide apart and the most beautiful sight in the world stands before us. "Wow!" says my brother. I cannot speak.

Four brand-new Douglas biplanes stand in a chorus line, wingtip to wingtip, their silver wings and navy blue fuselages shimmering, their burnished wood propellers in contrasting hue, their massive water cooled engines with their protruding exhaust stacks grimacing at us. Far to the rear, relegated to the outer shadows, we see two old De Havilland Fives observing the scene jealously.

"Brand new!" Wes chortles, "Brand god-damned new and I'm taking the first one out tonight!"

We assemble in the pilot's ready room with its six lockers, each with a pilot's name taped to the door. I look at the names….Smith, Chandler, Hill, Ames…. Ames? "But I thought Ames got killed."

"Shut up!" my brother says savagely, and then he is instantly sorry. My eyes fill with tears. Wes puts a paw around me and I am the center of their concern.

"Yes, Winfield," he says with great gentleness, "Ames was killed on this run."

He looks at my brother and shrugs. A look passes between them.

"But how?"

"He ran into a mountain over Bellefonte." There is a silence. No one feels comfortable. Then there is a ripping sound as Axel tears Ames' name off the locker door.

Wes strips to his boxer shorts. He pulls on a blue-veined set of long johns. Then he pulls on a pair of thick-ribbed hockey socks which he rolls down just below the knee. Over this goes a pair of olive drab army trousers. He tucks in a woolen army shirt and finally covers all of this with fur lined coveralls which sport a massive fleece collar. He sweeps his helmet and goggles from the shelf and, with much growling, pulls them on.

Now, we wait.

Outside, the mechanics have wheeled the Douglas on to the tarmac in front of the hanger. Huge wooden chocks are placed in front of each massive solid rubber tire. One mechanic mounts the toe steps to the cockpit and settles in, his greasy forage cap looking somehow out of place even for a Knight's Squire.

Now from offstage comes a dinky little mail truck, chuffing along in ridiculous contrast to the Mastodon crouched above it. A hastily lettered sign proclaims US MAIL and we see now that it is a converted delivery truck with the fish market's identity barely obscured by the hasty paint job. My attention is suddenly diverted as I see six mechanics form a line, hand in hand, to the left of the propeller:

"Off and closed!" one shouts.

"Off and closed!" comes a muffled shout from the cockpit.

"Contact!"

"Contact!"

Then, still hand in hand, all six on signal break into a dead run. Each flashes by the propeller except the last man. He grabs the prop blade, and this tug, coupled with the weight and momentum of the others, drags the blade in a clock wise whirl. There is a second pause, then a sharp bang. Smoke belches from the exhaust stacks and the engine blasts.

You can't hear us, but we are all cheering. Then the engine falters and begins to sputter. We groan. But then it catches to a full-throated roar which this time stays constant. We are home free. The mechanic eases the throttle back and the engine ticks, each RPM causing the plane to shake with expectancy, like a bronco in the chute.

Wes slaps my brother on the back, cuffs me gently, and shrugs into his parachute harness. Then he is out the door, hoisting his chute pack up against his ass as he waddles clumsily toward the plane. Halfway out the floodlights pick him up. Boosted by the mechanic, he mounts the toe steps, swings one leg and then the other into the cockpit and settles in with a mighty whoosh.

The mechanic drops off the lowest step and high tails it for the hanger. Two others flit in under the knifing prop and snap the chocks away. Wes twists in the cockpit and looks our way. With his helmet strapped under his chin and his goggles down, he is a grotesque gargoyle. He raises his arm and for the first time we see a long white scarf snapping in the slip stream. He guns her and the plane begins to move. Slowly, applying a little more throttle, he inches her off the tarmac and onto the grass. The wings rock crazily when he hits the rough. He opens her up a little more and taxis out past the flare pots and then suddenly he is gone in the darkness.

We hear him applying short bursts of power as he fishtails gently from side to side so he can see the flare markers which will indicate to him where he is to turn about and begin his takeoff run. There is a pause. He is turning forty-five degrees now and will run up his engine. There it is. We hear the engine sound rise higher as the RPMs increase. He is checking the engine magnetos. Right mag; okay. Left mag; okay.

Now the noise suddenly drops. He is turning, lining himself up for the takeoff run. And then we hear it: Full power…. Balls out….The sound of the US AIR MAIL. The sound builds and builds, but we still can't see him. And then, for a frozen instant, he flashes through the floodlights a few feet off the ground, pulls up sharply and is gone, with only the twinkling exhausts evidence that he was ever here.

Wes made it to Cleveland that night and many nights after that. He was the last of the old Hadley pilots and he finally surrendered to the Douglas DC3, forerunner of every airliner in the world and a plane he grew to love.

In 1936 he survived a crash in Chicago that left him with a twisted arm, grounded him permanently and broke his spirit and his heart.

I remember our last reunion....It took place in 1942. I was kid Army Air Corps pilot with brand new shiny wings; just graduated and the most dangerous of all pilots, because I knew *everything.* Wes was sitting alone in the half-darkness of his den when I came in. He looked tired and there were dark rims around his eyes that he didn't get from an open cockpit. He hadn't flown in six years and his face and body showed it. Something had died.

We talked about flying far into the night and we got more than a little drunk, but his eyes were on fire and he knew exactly what he was saying. He asked me thousands of questions about power settings, flaps, glide ratios, aerobatics and God knows what else.

Then it was time for me to go. He grabbed my hand in what once had been a great paw and looked into me:

"Good luck, Winfield, come back."

"Yes," I said.

"I won't be here," he said.

"I know," I said.

DIALOGUE

The man and his son had been driving across the desert floor for three hours. When they saw the "Beer on Tap" sign, they pulled up at the cafe. The door stuttered as they entered. A mass of dead flies trapped between the screens dropped to the floor. They hesitated, then took stools at the bar.

"Yeah?"

"Two beers, please."

"He old enough?"

"He's twenty-two."

"You from L.A., right?"

"That's right."

"Figures."

"What?"

But the bartender had already moved off. The man glanced at his son. The boy sat quietly, staring at his glass.

"I wonder what he meant by that?" His son said nothing.

The man ran his palm along the lip of the bar. "Look at this….hasn't used a clean rag in weeks. Here, smell."

The boy dipped his lips into the foam. He did not look at his father.

"This whole place smells. Come on, drink up. Let's get the hell out of here."

Now the bartender was standing directly in front of them. "Got a problem, mister?"

"No, what do I owe you?"

"Five dollars."

"Here."

"I can't change that."

"What do you mean?"

"I mean I can't change that."

"But it's only a twenty."

"I can see what it is."

"You mean you really can't?"

"I told you."

"But you haven't looked in the register."

"I don't have to."

"You mean you've had so many customers in here that you're out of change?"

"Nobody's been in here."

"And there's absolutely nothing in the register?"

"I told you."

"What about you? You got any singles in your pocket?"

"I can't help you, mister."

"But that's the smallest I've got."

"Maybe the kid's got some money."

"No, he hasn't got anything on him."

"That figures."

"Well, what are we going to do?"

"That's your problem."

"O.K. then, I'll write you a check."

"No checks."

"Maybe you'll accept credit cards in this wonderful place."

"Nope. We don't honor none of them."

"For god sakes man, what the hell do you want me to do?"

The bartender placed his rag in front of the man. "There's a gas station on the highway further out. You can get change there."

"How far?"

"Near."

"How far is near?"

"Five miles."

"Five miles!"

"You heard me."

"O.K., O.K., O.K., anything to get this settled. Come on, let's go!"

"Wait a minute."

"Now what?"

"Your kid stays here till you get back,"

"Now wait just one minute!"

"No, you wait a minute mister. I'm tired of your shit. You owe me for those beers and you're gonna pay and your kid stays right here to make damn sure you come back!"

The man rose slowly. He folded the bill and placed it in his wallet. At the door he turned.

"Wait here till I get back."

The boy sat quietly, staring at his empty glass. He could hear his father's stool still spinning. After a time he shifted slightly. Slowly he slid his hand into the pocket of his jeans and for the hundredth time, fingered the solitary five-dollar bill.

SUMMER STREET

Hagenbeck/Wallace
Sells/Floto
Ringling Brothers
Barnum and Bailey

These were the great circuses of the 30's that descended on our sleepy southern New England town every summer, unleashing a glittering galaxy of clowns, elephants, acrobats, trapeze artists, lions, tigers, brass bands, steam calliopes, midgets, bearded ladies, snake charmers, and assorted freaks, popcorn, peanuts, cotton candy, crackerjack, fizzy orange pop, hot dogs and much, much more.

We kids were always the first to spot the signs heralding the circus' approach, for, at dawn on a blazing, humid June morning, we awoke to see the first posters. One minute there was nothing, and then they would miraculously appear. Overnight the whole town would be blanketed. Every wall, fence, telephone pole, bus station and trolley stop would be plastered with the following message:

SELLS/FLOTO CIRCUS!!
SATURDAY, JUNE 10

SEE –
JUMBO, THE GREATEST PACHYDERM IN THE WORLD!
THE FLYING CODONNAS – DEATH-DEFYING TRAPEZE
ARTISTS!

SEE –

CLYDE BEATTY, LION TAMER! HOLDING SIX FOAMING BEASTS AT BAY

SEE –

FREE PARADE DOWN SUMMER STREET STARTING AT 10:00AM!

COME ONE, COME ALL!

And come we did, lining the street as the parade rumbled by, past the World War I monument on the Town Green, past the Town Hall, the Police Station, the Strand Theater, the Palace Theater and the Ferguson Library.

But the parade was almost an anticlimax for Jack and me, for we had already awakened at dawn and pedaled our bikes to the freight yard to greet the circus at 4:00am. We watched scores of huge elephants, guided by their cursing trainers, moving tons of wagons and cages and other heavy equipment. It was awesome, we watched enthralled. Then we raced back to the huge lot back in town to watch the birth of the circus.

It was then we made our fateful decision. We decided to offer our services to the circus in exchange for two free passes to the matinee performance. We need not have bothered, for we were suddenly accosted by a huge, bearded, heavily tattooed roustabout.

"You kids wanna" work for a free ticket?" he asked amiably.

"Sure," we swaggered.

"OK," he said, "follow me!"

He herded us toward the elephants. Then, abruptly, his mood changed. "Get the hell over there and start watering those elephants," he snarled.

And so it was that we labored; hour after hour, toting two huge pails of water from a nearby pond, endlessly, back and forth, back and forth. It was back-breaking, lung-burning work, always with the roustabout snarling and snapping at our heels.

That afternoon, in 90 degree heat, we sat under the Big Top in the worst seats available, too tired to really enjoy the show.

"Gee, Jack, this is swell," I said, with zero enthusiasm.

"Yeah," he said, and nodded off on the spot.

Jack and I went to every circus that came to town that magical summer. But, we *never, ever* worked for a free pass again. Instead we sold lemonade at a makeshift stand on the circus lot and came up with the cash to buy the best seats available under the Big Top.

We had learned a major lesson: AVOID MANUAL LABOR AT ALL COSTS (a philosophy that has stayed with me all my life).

And when the summer wound down, Jack and I once again mounted our bikes and set out to the railroad yard to bid the circus goodbye. There we stood on a pile of railroad ties, watching the train slide out, heading for the circus' Florida winter quarters. The engine chugged, the whistle shrilled a mournful farewell, as, waving forlornly, we watched our childhood, our innocence, and our dreams, slide slowly, but inexorably into the night.

GREYLOCK REVISITED

I stand again
On Greylock's brow
Breath burning
From the steep ascent

I see again
The languorous vista
That marks
The monarch's
Southern slope

No walled-in trails
With pickets
Flashing by
My chattering skis

Instead
A woman's perfumed waist
And sweet extended thighs

The snow creaks with cold
My nostrils stick
The globules freeze
And my eyes
Are diamonds

Everything glitters
Shimmers
The downward plunge begins
My companions and I
In trail

The snow boils
Over my skis
Engulfs my ankles
In wintry surf

We fan apart
Our hands touch
And we are geese
Or a handful of jacks
Cast upon the latticework

We are descending
Into the timberline
And each of us departs
The other
To explore
The scented caverns of pine

I lean into
The deeper shadow
Of powder blue

And then
Suddenly
A whir of wings
Explodes between my legs

And balance deserts me
My aplomb is gone
And I fight for it

With flailing hands
And quavering knees

The pheasant trumpets,
I recover,
And I am safe

I laugh in relief
Silvery
In sheer joy
The decibels repeat
Me! Me! Me!

A flash of sunlight
Frees me
And it is as if
I have burst through
An oaken door

Then my pace slows
And I am reunited
With my friends

We cast aside
Our gloves and poles

And glide the final lap
Shouting
And caroling
With flashing smiles
And scarlet faces
Staggering
And finally collapsing
In joy

For each of us
Is in the high noon

Of our life
And we are drunk with youth
And with what
Has just transpired

I stand again
On Greylock's brow
And see again
The languorous vista
That marks
The monarch's southern slope

I have a kinship now
With this magic place
Its wintry mark
Is upon my hair
And on my face

As now
With faded eyes
And plodding pace

I see today
What was
Yesterday's
Tomorrow

note: *Greylock Mountain, Commonwealth of Massachusetts*

INTERMISSION RIFF

The musicians mounted the bandstand and began unpacking their instruments. The trumpet players had an easy time of it. All they had to do was unpack their case, shove in the mouthpiece and they were ready to tune up. The sax men took out their horns and screwed in the mouthpiece. Adjusting the reed took a little longer, and they were constantly wetting it with their tongues; testing its bite. The bass player screwed his pegs back and forth and started scratching his balls. The piano man had it the easiest. He just flopped on his ass and was ready to go.

But the poor drummer; I would see him come on the stand a good hour before the rest of the band arrived for the one-nighter. He would beat a path back and forth between the ballroom and the bus, lugging huge black cases with the name "Shelly Manne, Stan Kenton Orchestra," stenciled on each. He would start unpacking and setting up, and if I was very lucky, I'd get a nod to help him.

First to emerge from the cocoon would be the bass drum, its main body gilded mother-of-pearl with the legend SLINGERLAND in bold black script on the front head. Shelly would scurry around, attach the bass pedal, slam his foot on it and my anticipating ears would be rewarded by a gorgeously deep boom. Next came the cymbals, shimmering and hissing as Shelly attached them to their mounts and stroked them tentatively with his wire brushes.

Then the tom-toms; there were three of them; two attached to the bass drum and one on three legs on the floor. Shelly would hover over them like a Vegas dealer and he'd insert his tuning key into the rim frets, cock his head like a robin sighting a worm, and make hair-line adjustments as he thrummed each with a felt mallet. While he was stroking the toms, my mind's eye would conjure up Mosques and Minarets, Sinbad Carpets and Harem Girls.

In those days all bands wore uniforms. Now, the guys wear faded blue jeans, tee shirts and Nikes, but then, bands were different, and Stan's band had a distinct look. The guys could have been doctors or stock brokers or Madison Avenue advertising executives. Each sported a coal-black Brooks Brothers suit, white button down Oxford shirt and a black knit tie. Only their shoes shouted their independence and marked them as musicians with individuality.

A dazzling mélange of footwear emerged from their trouser bottoms. The only requirement as far as Stan's Road Manager was concerned, was that they be black, in keeping with the rest of the ensemble. Ankle-high Italian boots with glinting gold buckles and pointed toes, black suede bucks with silvered laces, snakeskin Texas-Tom boots with girlish high heels, penny loafers with a needle thin scarlet stripe on the uppers, and God knows what else covered their feet.

Only Stan deviated; for while his uniform was semi-formal and in keeping with the tenor of the band, his attire said "LEADER" loud and clear. Stan probably had a hundred suits, half of which were always in the back of the bus. And tonight he had chosen a fawn-grey Glenn plaid, with a pencil striped tab collar shirt and a flowing waterfall of a tie colored robin's egg blue.

Cuff links flashed when he raised his arms for the down beat and his Cuban-heeled Cordovan leather shoes stomped out the tempo:

"All right, now here it is.

One, two, three, four;

Two, two, three, four!"

The Stan Kenton band has stayed with me through the years and will remain imbedded in my psyche for the rest of my life.

In good times, in bad times, in times of great joy, in times of sadness and, in times of terror and helplessness, these sounds marched through my brain and I would hear, over and over, the litany of the brass. It's gotten so that if I'm sitting in a boring business meeting, I can trip out, snap on the tape, and listen to the band for awhile, returning to reality precisely as my name is called for a comment. Suffice it to say that the

Kenton band has seen me through World Wart II, two marriages and one divorce, four kids, three firings and the purchase of three homes.

Listening to the band was an experience. In the first place, Stan's band was the loudest in the world (you either hated it or you loved it, there was no middle ground), and when it played fortissimo, with five trumpets and five trombones blowing, it was unique. When the brass section hit an entrance on open horns, the effect was electric. If you stood in front of the band as close to the brass section as possible, as I always did, you could feel the shock wave. It was a wall of sound and your ears would sing with the decibels.

I first heard the Kenton band while I was having sex with a girl in the back seat of my Dad's Essex Terraplane. The radio in the front seat was at low ebb, but in the middle of our gymnastics, I caught the announcer's introduction:

"Ladies and gentlemen, from the beautiful Rendezvous Ballroom overlooking fabulous Balboa Island in sunny Southern California, new music from a new gentleman from the Golden State, the music of Stanley Kenton and his orchestra…."

The band broke into Stan's later famous theme, "Artistry in Rhythm" and rendered me impotent for the moment. I was temporarily out of ardor.

"What's the matter, Winnie?" she asked.

"Shut up! I wanna' hear this!"

"See, I knew you'd be that way (pause) afterwards."

"Naw, Mary Lou, it ain't that, it's just that band…"

"But you said you'd still respect me…"

"I do, I do, I do!"

"Then why?"

"Mary Lou, please shut up. I'll respect you in a minute!"

During World War II, the band was piped to those of us who were in Europe, via V discs that were spun by the Army and Air Force disc jockeys on American Forces Radio Network. I made a vow that if I lived through all that shit I would seek out and listen to the Kenton band the moment I set foot in the states.

This got to be an obsession with me and I told everybody in my outfit who would listen what I was going to do when I got home. I would corner guys when I was really juiced and fill their ear ad nauseam. It got so bad that it spilled over into my time in combat:

I was point man on a patrol sent ahead of our main body to scout a clump of German farmhouses on the outskirts of a ruined village deep in the Ruhr. Fanned out, bristling with caution, we all hit the dirt simultaneously when a Kraut machine gun opened up on us. Art Vogel and I rolled behind a cluster of boulders, cursing, jamming our helmets into the dirt. Bullets cracked a hair breadth away and ricochets searched us with an evil whine. We lay there, pinned down, face to face. After a while, the machine gun shifted its fire to a target down the road and we were temporarily safe. Art leaned toward me:

"You were singing," he said incredulously.

"I was?"

"Yeah, what the fuck was it?"

"Stan Kenton's theme."

"You're nuts!"

I rolled over on my back. "Art," I vowed, "if I ever get out of this and get back to the States, I'm gonna go straight to where the band is playing, I'm gonna get drunk as a bastard and stand right in front of the band. And you know what else I'm gonna do?"

"What?"

"I'm gonna let that brass section knock me right flat on my ass!"

Well, it's deeds that count, not words, because when I got back to the States I didn't rush out and seek the Kenton band. I got married first and started a family and a career, but one night I was in Los Angeles on a business trip and I was sitting at the bar of the Statler Hotel, a young Turk from the East with a boring evening laid out in front of me like a frayed carpet.

The year was 1955. I leaned over to the bartender:

"Is there any good jazz in town?"

"I can getcha' a girl right here in the hotel, I gotta' connection."

"No, no, no, jazz…..jazz music!"

"Oh," he paused. "Well, let's see, there's someone named Stanley Kenton at the Crescendo on the Strip."

"Let me have my check."

"Was it something I said?"

But I was gone.

The band was just coming on the stand when I arrived. I argued with the Captain for a table in front of the brass section and I tipped him so outrageously that he outdid himself. He placed a chair in front of the ringside table. When the trombone slides were full extended, I could feel little sprays of spit. It was marvelous.

Stan had a trumpet man named Jack Sheldon whom I had never heard before. He played the jazz choruses with a rich, fuzzy tone punctuated with slurs, ripping arpeggios and a fat vibrato. I also heard a guy named Maynard Ferguson, then a kid, with an absolutely iron lip. His range was so great that he seemed unreal. He was an animal, an absolute freak who played all the screech-horn parts. The band would be blasting away on the final chorus of something and you could hear Maynard way up there all alone in the stratosphere without an oxygen mask.

When the band broke for intermission, I asked Stan to join me at my table, introduced myself, and we talked. I invited him to have a drink at my hotel. He accepted, but suggested his Beverly Hills home instead. We talked jazz till the room grew pale with morning, and later, still half drunk and in total euphoria, I stumbled into a sales meeting at the hotel just before I was due to make the new product marketing presentation.

It had taken me over ten years, but I had found a lifetime symbol.

When Stan Kenton died in 1979, I said to my wife:

"Well, the old man is gone, and you know something? He was a complete, bona fide hero to me. I loved him."

"Well, honey," she said, "If you wanted a hero, you sure picked the right man."

DOC

Eric Hord, otherwise known as Doc, was a study in extremes. He lived on the edge, and his sips from the cup of life were alternately sweet, bitter, sublime, terrifying and finally, terminal. Caught in the throes of his ever-changing lifestyle, he steered a perilous course throughout his entire life. If ever there was a person who subscribed wholeheartedly to the doctrine, "If it's not worth doing to the extreme, it's not worth doing at all," it was Doc.

And I loved him dearly.

For me, it all began when I was on the periphery of Doc's friendship with my son, Jim. Both were musicians, both were guitarists, and, as time passed, both became close friends. Through Jim I learned of Doc's fame as a guitar virtuoso with the Mamas and the Papas, which I found impressive. But it wasn't until I heard him play and sing that I got hooked on him – permanently.

I remember him tilting back in his chair, squinting in the sun, then playing and singing the song that defined him, defined my son, and defined me. It is called, "In Your Mind." I have never heard anything like it since, and I never will. It's lovely haunting, heart-breaking, yet joyous melody has never left me. And when Jim sings it now, I hear Doc's voice.

So began a deep and lasting friendship between us. Doc lived (out of his car, literally) in San Diego, and most every weekend he would make the long trek to Studio City to visit me. He'd pull up out front. I'd hear the gears rasp and I'd think, "Oh shit, he's just dropped the transmission (which incidentally, never failed him). Then guitar in hand, he'd plop down on my den couch, light up a joint, blow a puff in my face to tease me, and then in his rasping voice, greet me with warmth and affection.

"Get that fucking Rams game on – NOW!" he'd bark.

Both Doc and I were, in those days, rabid Rams football fans; first when they were in Los Angeles, and then when they moved to St. Louis. We both had been long suffering – but not now; for this was 1999 and the Rams were a red-hot high-scoring touchdown machine that would, in that glorious season, win the Super Bowl.

These were golden afternoons, the game moving to its happy conclusion, the late afternoon sun, casting a wan winter light. Sylvia, always there, softly touching each of us, as she poured the thick, black, fragrant coffee.

Doc and I covered a lot of ground during those long afternoons. We swapped lies, told boastful tales of derring-do, and generally carried on like giggling kids. He told me many tales about his life, some crude, some preposterous, some fall-down funny and some I wish he had never told me. Like this one:

Doc told me he was in New York City a number of years ago, gigging around and not making a dime because everything he earned from gigs went straight into a floating fund to support his heroin addiction….and he was into it, big time.

Finally, when he got kicked out of a place to sleep, he wandered the streets, sleeping in parks and in stair wells, anywhere, everywhere and nowhere; an endless journey. Until one winter night, he found himself standing in front of a Catholic Church somewhere downtown, near the battery.

For a long time he stood in the shadow, and then Doc mounted the steps of the church and entered a new life. But not before he experienced hell on earth. When he rang the bell, the Mother Superior herself answered the door. Recognizing his addiction, she took him in, which was saintly. He would pay dearly for this new life. She led him to a solitary room, ushered him inside and told me she would help him kick his heroin habit.

Her technique for helping him to kick was the work of the devil. For, as Doc tells it:

"She locked me in this room for 34 days. She told me before she locked me in, that I would kick it; that I would see and feel the fires of hell first, but in the end, I would be clean. She said that was her promise to me before God….and she lived up to it. I became a screaming maniac while I was kicking. Everyday she'd come to see me, fend me off, and leave hot meals for me. I was insane. It was terrible."

But in the end, depleted physically, morally and spiritually, Doc, with the firm, unwavering support of the Mother Superior, grasped the first rung of the rest of his life.

It would be nice if I could say that Doc moved into a new life that would bear some semblance of sanity or purpose, but such was not the case. But there were occasional bright spots nevertheless. For example:

Doc took a deep interest in my son, Jim, not only as a musician, but as a man. He followed Jim's formation of "The Gluey Brothers" band with deep interest, and he stood close by as Jim became a more skilled guitarist, drummer, song writer, vocalist and leader of the band. In short, Doc was always there for Jim. He taught Jim a lot more than guitar, and he gave the gift of his talent to my son willingly, lovingly and without expecting anything in return.

Then one night, as Doc and I were listening to the Gluey Brothers band kick off a set, I leaned over, "Doc," I asked, "you give Jim so much. Why?" Doc turned to me, jerking his thumb at Jim, who was deep into a guitar solo, "That's why," he said.

And then, one day, the phone rang. I picked up. There was a long silence….too long. A voice spoke from a great distance. I knew it was Doc. "I'm sick, they're giving me about three weeks," he said. "Oh," I said, as the receiver clicked off.

UNTITLED

the slope steepened
suddenly
and he glanced upward at his fear

above
he could make out
that which he was seeking

clearly visible
totally inaccessible
yet accessible
at the same time

in truth
he was alone
seeking that which he knew not
and
in his heart
that which he would never find

he searched
the bleakness
of his memory
a slate
on which nothing had been written

and nothing came
or would ever come

he did not know
how
or why
he became separated
from the main party
at ten thousand feet?
or twenty thousand feet?
the oxygen mask burning deeply
  (suck air)

he knew only that they were roped together
as they traversed
the black crevasses
each an endless
clarion call to infinity – eternity

and then he finally remembered
they were roped out
six of them
punching forward
with deep trepidation
their ice axes chipping
with agonizing slowness
  (suck air)

living
in but a second
an excruciating lifetime
  (suck air)

put one foot in front of another
  (suck air)

raise leaden arms

in supplication
drive the axe to its mark
    (suck air)

oxen in the yoke
herd in movement
    (suck air)

the voice said
"look back"
and he did so
viewing the centipede of tracks
that extended
back from base camp
to the final assault on the summit
their tracks bunched together
tribal
assured
    (suck air)

but
his tracks
a terror trail
away from the main body
bending recklessly
further
ever further from base camp
    (suck air)

blessed base camp
    (suck air)

base camp
with its scalding soup
tribal camaraderie
the layered sleep of near-death
the wind screaming

as they waited out the storm
    (suck air)

and when he saw the leopard
he felt no fear
for all of this was pre-ordained
the Sherpa had spoken
"life is infinite
and death
but an interruption
a gateway"
    (suck air)

the numbness in his mind
so long endured
now gave way
to the blinding white light
of total clarity
    (suck air)

for he remembered:
"on the summit of Kilimanjaro
they found
the frozen carcass of a leopard
no one ever knew
what the leopard was seeking
at that altitude"'

he looked up
the leopard was waiting
and as he moved
so moved the leopard
closer
ever closer
until his entire vision
his body
his very essence

moved deeply
into the animal
the beautiful leopard
and now
he felt nothing
but utter peace

* *This quote, loosely, is from the short story, "The Snows of Kilimanjaro," by Ernest Hemingway*

LITTLE OLD LADY FROM PASADENA

Prologue

If I had but known the sequence of unlikely events that would transpire on that wonderful Sunday afternoon, not only would I have joyously entered the church as I did, but I would also have rushed in shouting "halleluiah!" as well.

The date: *Sunday, November 12*
The time: *Mid afternoon*
The place: *Pasadena Presbyterian Church*
The occasion: *Performance by the Pasadena Boys Choir*
Age range: *8 to 12 years*
Voice range: *All sopranos*
Purpose: *My wife and I were there to hear our neighbor's young son sing in the choir*

If you have never heard a boys choir, do so, because, in a fleeting moment in time, these boy sopranos generate a beautiful, pure, sound.

It is the sound of innocence.

We moved forward, down the aisle, to a pew close to the choir. I slid in, settled down with a whoosh and leaned on my cane in anticipation.

I was not to be disappointed.

And then she slid in next to me; the little old lady from Pasadena. And here I make a correction. She was old, but not little. She was tall and patrician, a handsome woman. Her figure was lovely (which bespoke a lifetime of diet and exercise in swank gymnasiums). Her features were aquiline and cleanly drawn. A Pasadena aristocrat if there ever was one, her clothing regal, and contemporary.

She exuded class. She was royalty.

"Good afternoon Ma'am," I said, rising and extending my hand to help seat her.

"Good afternoon to you, sir," she replied, smiling warmly and taking my hand in a firm grip.

We began to converse, and we hit it off immediately. We laughed and joked, our conversation crackling between us like static electricity. We exchanged cards. We talked about our mutual love of the boys choir, of classical music and opera as well. And then, for some reason, I asked her:

"Do you like jazz?"

"Very much," she answered.

"Really? Whom do you like?" I ventured, figuring she'd give me Glenn Miller or some other tired old dance band from the thirties.

Never in a million years, was I prepared for her answer. She drew herself up to her full height.

"Dizzy Gillespie," she said, almost defiantly.

I was blown away!

"You what?" I almost shouted.

"Dizzy Gillespie," she repeated.

Side bar: Dizzy Gillespie, a genius, was an all time GREAT Bebop jazz trumpeter of the Bop era, given to unbelievably frantic, complex harmonic improvisation; hence the name Dizzy.

"You heard me," she smiled.

"But, but..."

"But, what? Think I'm too old, young man?"

"How old are you?"

"Ninety three!"

"Wow!"

"In fact, young man," she said, "Dizzy had great chops!"

Then the sound of the choir ended our conversation and I sank deeper into the cushions, my mind a wasteland of seemingly disconnected thoughts – like Dizzy's solos. Later, as I bent over to kiss her hand in farewell, she gave me a dazzling smile and floated out of the pew. The last I saw of her, a shaft of late afternoon sunlight lanced through the stained glass window, setting her sequined hair ablaze in a divine light.

Epilogue

I couldn't wait to go to the internet to place the order for a Dizzy Gillespie tee-shirt – color, black, white lettering, size small. I had them FedEx the shirt to her with this note:

"To the hip lady from Pasadena"

It was signed: "Love, Dizzy Gillespie."

THE HOUSE ON THE HILL

The wrench is man-sized and heavy
And I am clutching it in my tiny hands
It is an important errand
I am taking it to my father
Along with his battered Fedora
Which, placed on my head
Obscures most of my vision
He is standing beside his truck
In our long driveway that winds down from
The house on the hill

My father reaches down from his great height
And removes the Fedora
Takes the wrench and places his hand
On my tiny head
I feel the firm but gentle touch
Of his work-stained fingers
And his heartbeat is mine

I am standing before a field of daisies
Acres of them
All white, with delicate petals
And golden eyes
Swaying, dancing, bowing in the warm June breeze
I stand by my first-born son

His tiny trusting hand in mine
He is looking deeply into the golden haze
"Daisies," I say
"Day-dees," he says

My mother stands on the great front porch
Of the house on the hill
She is drying her hands on her apron
I get out of the car and come up the path
I am mounting the steps
I have been away a long, long time
And I have been in great danger
My step is halting
As I see the lines of pain and suffering
On her face
And then we embrace
And I am healed
And tears of blessed release
Course down my cheeks

The Atlantic surf is crashing
White plumed
Black depths
Icy spume
Trails threads of cold
It is November
And it is New England
And I am once again
Treading the beaches of my childhood
And another tiny, trusting hand
With a fiery red mitten
Nestles in my palm

The wind is snarling
The storm is imminent
But all is well
Because we both can look up and see
The house on the hill

She looks up at me, my daughter
Her tiny face, turned up nose
Pink cheeks and sparkling eyes
Her lips move
She says, "Daddy"
And smiles the sweetest smile, ever….ever

And now it is high summer
And the sound of the locust
Is everywhere
The heat is palpable
And there is a deep haze
She looks up at me….another daughter
And I see her golden hair
And her eyes, a reflection of the summer sky
She has her tiny lemonade stand
Beside this dusty country lane
The pitcher sweats
The ice tinkles
Like wind chimes
And she smiles
"Daddy"

And now I am walking another road again
My hair is white with winter's touch
And once again I am standing before
Another son
Watching, listening
His hands are all I can see
Above the cymbals
I am listening to the rhythmic patterns he plays
His flashing hands
Bring joy to my heart and tears to my eyes
He glances up, smiles that crooked jazz smile
"Hi Dad," he says

Spangles of light
Bounce with shimmering intensity
Off the pool surface
And you are in the pool
Striking about
With your thin, yet muscular arms and legs
Your tightly curled auburn hair
Reflects the summer sun
And you are in the high noon of your childhood

I sit down
And dangle my legs
In the warm water
The big Labrador
Who has been swimming with you
Mounts the steps
And shakes himself
A shudder that courses through his body and out his tail
You giggle with delight
"Boompa got wet!" you say
We laugh, and I place my hand gently on your shoulders
And I am filled with indescribable joy
For you are my dear grandson
An extension of me
And the house on the hill

FLIGHT THIRTEEN

"Good afternoon, ladies and gentlemen. This is your captain speaking. Welcome to Eastern Airline's flight 13 from Houston, Texas to Idyllwild Airport, New York City. We have leveled off at our cruising altitude, 30,000 feet. Our route today will take us over San Antonio, Oklahoma City, Kansas City, Nashville, Philadelphia and on into New York City. We are estimating landing in New York at 4:07 pm, Eastern Standard Time. The weather en route is mostly clear, with some cloud cover between Philadelphia and New York. So, sit back, relax, and enjoy the flight and thank you for flying Eastern Airlines."

I was sitting in the lounge at the rear of the plane, next to Ed Sullivan, host of the then wildly popular, top-rated CBS Television network Sunday variety show, "Toast of the Town." I was Ed's Road Manager and we had just come from a personal appearance at the Lone Star State Automobile Show at the brand new Shamrock Hotel in Houston. We were relaxing over a drink when the head stewardess approached us:

"Mr. Sullivan, Mr. Goulden, the Captain sends his compliments, and would like you to be his guests on the flight deck."

Now I must tell you that we were aboard a Lockheed Constellation, a four-engine, propeller-driven aircraft. You see, in 1955, there were no commercial jets, only prop planes and, at that time, the "Connie" was the queen of the skies.

We threaded our way to the flight deck and peered in. The flight crew consisted of three men: Captain, left hand seat, First Officer-Co-pilot, right hand seat, Flight Engineer, seated directly behind the co-pilot, facing a bewildering array of dials; one set for each of the plane's four engines.

During the introductions, the Captain, Dan Southard, mentioned that he lived in Wilton, Connecticut, and, when I said I did too, he grinned:

"Tell you what, Win, I'm parked at Idyllwild (now known as JFK), so you ride with me to Wilton and I'll drop you off."

"Great! Thanks Dan!" I said.

Then, as Ed Sullivan left the flight deck to go back to his seat, Dan said, "Win, stick around. Why don't you fly her for awhile?"

The co-pilot slid out of the right hand seat. I slid in and grasped the wheel. (I had been a pilot in World War II). As I settled in, I thought, "Jesus! If Ed Sullivan and the rest of the folks back there ever find out who is flying this crate right now....!"

So, here's the scenario: Everything is cool. I'm at the controls of a giant commercial airliner at 30,000 feet. The temperature outside is 30 below zero and we are over Philadelphia. And now, for the first time, I see thick, dark billowing clouds ahead – a solid undercast.

"OK, Captain," I grin, "time for you Pros to take over. Send the co-pilot back in."

Dan laughed: "OK, but stay with us Win, there's a small jump seat right behind my seat. Sit there."

Then it happened. The Flight Engineer broke in, "Captain, number two engine fuel pump is GONE!"

Dan twisted in his seat. "Jesus," he said, "I don't like this, I don't like this at all; feather #2."

I glanced out the tiny window and saw the prop on #2 engine stop turning. Dan had good reason to be concerned. When a fuel pump breaks, it sprays gasoline all over red hot cylinders. Dan spoke calmly, "Hit the flame retardant."

Then he turned to the co-pilot. "Call Idyllwild, I'm declaring an emergency, tell 'em we're coming right straight in."

Then he turned to the Flight Engineer. "Get back there and see if we're on fire," he said.

I was paralyzed with fright. Yet strangely calm. I had had these same feelings before.

We did not catch fire. We let down through a thick undercast and broke out to a wonderful sight – Runway 270, Idyllwild, New York City. As we touched down, fire trucks and emergency vehicles raced beside us all the way down the runway until we braked to a stop.

Later in the car with Dan, neither of us said much. Finally, he said, "Win, that was just routine."

"Oh right, sure," I said, "just routine."

He looked at me out of the corner of his eye.

I looked back at him and I said, "Bullshit!"

Then, we both roared with laughter. Dan stomped on the accelerator pedal and we burned rubber out of the parking lot.

WINTER DREAMS

I could always tell
I would wake up suddenly
Just at dawn
And I could sense it
I could feel it
I would smile sleepily
Shuffle to the window
Lift up the shade
And there it would be
Snowfall

And, as the sun's first rays
Turned the snow to gold
My entire universe lit up
As the silent majesty
Of my winter dreams
Unfolded

    The phone would ring at dawn and I'd hear Jack's voice: "Winnie, it's time!"

    I knew what that meant; time to break out the old Flexible Flyer sled and make a bee-line to the top of North Street hill, where Jack was waiting.

    North Street hill was over a mile long, a steep hill at the start, then softening into a gentle slope that offered us kids a great, long exhilarating ride, past Hart School and over the Rippowan River stone bridge, gliding to a reluctant stop.....smack dab in front of the Saint Andrews Church.

We would cluster at the top of the hill, form a line and when it was my turn to go, I would get an iron grip on my sled, and, after a dead run, simultaneously belly flop onto the sled and grab the steering bar. While all this was going on, my dog, Freckles, a flop-eared Springer Spaniel, would race alongside, barking like crazy, escorting me down the hill.

The town even cordoned off North Street hill so that we kids would be safe as we had our fun.

But we all paid a price for sledding on North Street, because after a glorious ride, dragging our sleds behind, we had to walk up a whole mile back to the top of North Street for another ride, and another, and another, until, in almost total darkness, we trudged home, apple-cheeked, dead tired, digging into Mom's apple fritters and pork chops with an appetite like a horse.

And, the very next day, we would all be back out there again. Norm DeVed, Christine Conron, and Russ Leibfarth, and Joe Iacovo, and Blanche Bogden,

Henry Zaaleskie,
Sis McCue,
Herb Reinenger,
Beverly Whitford,
Jacob Cohen,
Zelda Wakeman,
Ben Mead,
Mary Louise Scofield,
Bob Greeny,
Evelyn Dorflinger,
Larry Chimbole,
Ann Jankowitz,
Billy Barthrum,
Dody Wadhams,
Kenny Ballard.........

Epilogue

I dedicate this piece to the person who, as a kid, shared *all* of this with me – my boyhood chum and my lifelong friend, Jack Williamson, who, sadly, is in the last stages of Alzheimer's.

>BUT, you know what?
>I like to think,
>I like to think,
>that maybe,
>just maybe,
>Jack's having his winter dreams too.

POISON IVY

In the first place, New England is not a group of States. It is a state of mind. No one knows this better than me, because that's where I was born. The absolute personification of New England is the seaport of Marblehead, Massachusetts, placed like a jewel on the Atlantic's far shore, a wellspring of culture, tradition and the best grilled fresh-caught lobster in the world.

Marblehead is at its best, or at its worst, during the high noon of summer. It depends on your point-of-view. For while Marblehead braces in late fall for the harsh New England winter, it also braces in early summer for an invasion of tourists. You may like them, as many do. You may not like them, as many do, but you sure as hell can't ignore them. All residents of Marblehead know one thing; the town's economy depends on tourism, and everybody, from the smartly doffed real estate renter, to the grizzled fisherman, to the spectacled restaurateur, knows that their survival depends on tourism.

It was this atmosphere into which my wife, my boyhood chum and myself, were propelled one fine summer day in June. We were visiting Lannie, a family friend of long standing. She put us up in an old coach house, built in the year 1630, a massive structure with huge windows, peering approvingly at the teeming activities on Marblehead Bay.

Then came the night we attended a gala party at the Marblehead Bay Yacht Club, a magnificent edifice standing like a reproving sentinel at the entrance to the bay. Yachtsmen from all over were arriving by land and sea, the men in natty, formal yachting gear, the women in chic, exquisitely tailored designer gowns.

A haze of perfumed splendor hung over the entire assemblage, unfolding in all its wealth and pageantry. BMWs, Mercedes, Jags, and an occasional Rolls Royce churned the parking lots. Uniformed chauffeurs abounded and the place was one seething mass of activity. For some reason, this parade of opulence, privilege and wealth made me somewhat uneasy. Because, in the back of my mind, I remembered the Ivy League syndrome: Fathers who graduated from Yale, Harvard or Princeton pledged their financial contributions to their respective Alma Maters. They also pledged their sons, who were barely out of grammar school. It was understood that the sons would follow their father's into the cloistered academia that is the Ivy League.

Lannie moved into the club with Sylvia, Jack and I in tow. The band was already on the stand, cranking out the syrupy sounds of Guy Lombardo. The place was packed and you could smell the perfume, sweat and stale champagne of Saturday night.

"Let me introduce you to the Commodore," Lannie said, tapping him on the shoulder. He turned then, eyeballing us up and down. He was handsome, dark-haired and deeply tanned. He wore a navy-blue gold-buttoned blazer with the yacht club coat-of-arms embroidered over the left breast. A navy tie, white shirt, white shoes and knife creased white flannel trousers completed his ensemble.

Good evening," he said, and Lannie introduced us. Then came the first probe:

"And where do you live?" he asked.

"Los Angeles."

"Los Angeles?" he said, his upper lip curling ever so slightly. "I was there once," he continued, "the traffic was abominable. How can you live in such a place?"

"We live in a suburb," Sylvia said.

"And where might that be?"

"North Hollywood."

"North Hollywood!" he laughed, now clearly showing his disdain, and it was then that I realized that he was quite drunk, in that controlled state of drunkenness that New Englanders strive to maintain.

Then he swiveled his guns on me. "Are you a college graduate? You did go to college didn't you?"

"Yes, I graduated from Rutgers."

"Rutgers?"

"Yes, Rutgers."

He paused, as if searching his memory. "Rutgers, Rutgers…..oh yes, yes….a nice little college in New Jersey. Yes."

A great rage boiled up in me. I was weak with anger and I peered at him through a red haze. I had to retaliate. I knew I would regret it tomorrow if I did not.

As he turned to leave, I swung him around. "Sir," I said, my words strangled, "You know what they taught me at Rutgers? Something Harvard never taught you."

"And what, my good man, is that?"

"Manners," I said, turning on my heel.

As I walked out, I saw again through my tears, my mother crying softly in the breakfast nook of our home, clutching my father's meager pay envelope. I saw my blue collar father holding me in his arms, and I saw the maid we had disappear. I saw our cars vanish and I saw the furniture being sold as the Great Depression spread throughout our hometown like an oil slick, sparing no one, affecting everyone.

For I felt no satisfaction in responding to his insults, no sense of having "told-off that son-of-a-bitch," only a deep, deep sadness, which I still feel, and for which there will never be an antidote.

MILITARY INTELLIGENCE

Time: *World War II*
Date: *April 1943*
Place: *Victorville, California*
        Glider Pilot Airborne Training Unit
        Deep in the Mojave high desert

Scene: A formation of Sergeants, including me, waiting for the Lieutenant to drill us.

Shtick: We had an infamous phrase called "famous last words", which we used constantly. If we did use it, it would invoke the gravest consequences if delivered to one of greater rank. Here are some examples:

> "Fuck you General. *You* attack that beach!"
> > or
> "Fuck you, Captain, I'm not doin' guard duty tonight!"
> > or
> "Fuck you Sir, I am *not* jumping out of this airplane!"

All of these, of course, were delivered only amongst ourselves. We had contests in the barracks to see who could come up with the zaniest "famous last words."

As I said before, I was standing in that formation of sergeants waiting for the arrival of Lieutenant Pierce, who was nowhere to be seen. So, I opened my stupid trap and bellowed, "Fuck you Lieutenant, we're not gonna' drill today!"

There was dead silence. Absolute dead silence. Nobody, and I mean nobody, laughed.

Then from behind the formation came an answering bellow. "Oh, fuck you Lieutenant, is it?! You, Goulden!" he barked, jamming his finger at me. "Haul your ass! On the double!"

He hustled me away. And then, behind us, all the men collapsed in laughter.

"Sir, I can explain," I said lamely, standing at attention.

"Don't bother!" he snapped. We were face to face.

"Smart ass, huh?!"

"Yes, sir!"

"Goulden!" he glared.

"Sir?"

"I was a Sergeant before I was a Lieutenant. Enlisted men are supposed to hate officers. I know I did. Now, get your ass back in that formation. And, today, Sergeant, *you* will drill the men!"

Epilogue

Fast forward one year to June, 1944. Infantry combat in France. A German machine gun opens up on the beach. I'm caught in the open. I dive into a foxhole. It's already occupied. I pile in anyway. On top of – you guessed it, Lieutenant Pierce. He looks up at me, but now I'm a Captain. I outrank him!

And he says, "Fuck you Captain, dig your *own* foxhole!"

I never saw him again.

DUKE'S MIXTURE

About a thousand years ago, when I was a student at Rutgers University in my senior year, I took a class in Music appreciation. Most seniors took it because it was an easy point toward graduation.

But not me.

The professor was a man named F. Austin Campbell, whom we immediately nick-named "Soup." I loved Soup. He was a young man, intelligent, articulate and totally dedicated to classical music.

When the class convened three days a week, Soup would play a vast recorded array of Beethoven, Bach, Brahms, Wagner and many others. While the majority of the class was bored, I was dazzled by all this; so much so that I would spend hours after class listening to the masters again and again.

Then came the day when Soup introduced us to Igor Stravinsky. I took to Stravinsky like a duck takes to water, for within his compositions, which were atonal, polytonal, both strident and melodic, I heard the phrasings of Duke Ellington, one of my big jazz heroes.

When I told Soup about the crossover between Stravinsky and Duke Ellington, he paused, pondered, then gave me a long, intense look.

"Win," he said, "you may have something there."

Neither of us could have forecast what was about to take place, but both of us knew instinctively that something had forever changed in our relationship and a bond had been forged between us.

Then one day, out of a clear blue sky, he called me over:

"Goulden."

"Yes, Sir."

"You like jazz, don't you?"

"Well, sir, sort of…"

"What do you mean, 'sort' of? You love jazz!"

He leaned closer. "Starting next Friday, and every Friday thereafter, you, Mr. Goulden, will take the last 15 minutes of my class and lecture on Jazz."

"But, but…."

"No buts."

"But what will I do?"

"For starters, pick stuff from your own jazz record collection and tell the class about what you will be playing. Once you get going, you'll do fine. Let your love of jazz prevail."

"And one more thing," he said, "The class just might learn something about jazz." He paused, "I know I will," he said. Then he was gone.

Soup was right. I did think of something. Every Friday I got my 15 minutes of fame, playing jazz records and explaining to the class my choices of artists and styles – always under the smile of Soup. So the relationship between Professor and student blossomed, flowered, and flourished.

Soup took me to New York to Carnegie Hall to see and hear the London Symphony. I took him to a dive in Greenwich Village to hear Louis Armstrong. All of this, mind you, on his tab. (In those days there were no cover charges and a scotch and soda cost 35 cents. It was a cultural exchange of monumental proportions).

Then what transpired next led me to the greatest evening of my young life.

Colleges and universities up and down the East Coast held classical concert series in which internationally known symphony orchestras performed. These events were strongly supported and well attended by both students and the general public as well. But, in my eyes, the concerts were conventional and very dull. Where were the modern composers like Stravinsky, Schoenberg, Milhaud? Where was jazz, a truly American art form? And why not jazz? Why not Duke Ellington?

In an editorial in the University newspaper I ranted: "It is time Rutgers University should include in its concerts the music of Edward Kennedy Ellington – NOW!"

Several weeks later, in class, Soup met me at the door, waving my editorial.

"All right wise guy!"

"What?"

"You'll get your wish."

"What do you mean?"

"The University Concert Series Board of Directors has extended an invitation to Mr. Ellington and his orchestra to appear on a concert series evening and Mr. Ellington has accepted.

Wow!" I shouted, "That's great! Really great!!"

Soup leaned forward, "Oh, and one more thing."

"What?"

"You, Winfield Goulden, are going to be the Master of Ceremonies!"

And so it came to pass that one night, in the Rutgers University gymnasium, I found myself, all 20 years of me, clad in white tie and tails, moving out in front of the Duke Ellington Orchestra, about to introduce Duke himself.

Soup introduced me. Then I introduced Duke. I was electrified. And I was, as Duke himself later remarked, "One cool cat."

After I graduated in 1941, life, history and World War II swallowed me up and Soup and I lost touch.

Years later, on a beautiful autumn, Sunday afternoon, once again on the Rutgers Campus, life came full circle for me. I had just married my beautiful Sylvia and I took her to New Brunswick to see the Rutgers Campus. It was there that I heard the deep, resonant surge of the Kirkpatrick Chapel pipe organ.

We entered the empty chapel. A wall of sound enveloped us. We were transformed into another world; the stiff-backed pews, the murky oil paintings of long-forgotten founding fathers glaring down at us, the sun lancing through the stained glass windows, and the organ playing Bach's "Fugue and Toccata in D Minor."

The rafters shook. And then it was silent. Sylvia and I applauded. I looked up – and froze. There, no longer a young man, white-haired and bespectacled stood "Soup" Campbell.

"Hey Soup!" I shouted, the tears welling.

He looked down at me, peering through the years. Then he lit up. And a broad smile transformed him.

"Hey Duke!!" he shouted, as we fell into each others arms.

Coda

Again, years passed. The last time Sylvia and I saw Duke Ellington and his orchestra was for his Sacred Concert in Los Angeles. After the gig, Duke adjourned to a community room adjacent to the church.

A chair had been placed on a platform in the middle of the room and Duke ascended his 'throne'. Sylvia stood in front of the throne. "I love you Duke," she said, blowing him a kiss. Duke extended a hand, inviting Sylvia to sit on his lap. Then, a multitude of equally attractive women pressed forward and clustered around him.

With a beautiful smile, Duke surveyed his harem and said:

"We love you madly."

TWELVE

When it came to jury duty, my philosophy had always been, "Never present a stationary target." Through the years, I adhered faithfully to this philosophy, always returning each summons with a highly creative laundry list of reasons why it would be absolutely impossible for me to serve. I should have known better, because one day I cast these constraints to the wind and responded to the summons with an emphatic YES!

To this day, I have never figured out what motivated me, but one morning I found myself in a downtown LA courthouse, buried to my eyeballs in a jury pool of a million characters, one of whom would ultimately lead me into a labyrinth of fractured legalese, abject frustration and pure hatred. I'll call him Horace.

The case we jurors had was this: A young couple, who were living together, had a big fight and split. She fled the apartment they shared in a rage, leaving all her clothing and valuables behind. He, in a savage mood, was alleged to have set fire to the clothes she left behind and trashing all her valuables as well.

She was suing him for destroying her entire wardrobe, leaving her literally with only the clothes on her back. The trial lasted two days, and we, the jury finally got the case for deliberation.

We filed from the courtroom into the jury room. The bailiff closed the door. We took seats at a long table. And?? Nothing happened. No one spoke. There was some fidgeting, but otherwise, silence. Everyone looked at their counterpart facing them across the table; still dead silence.

Finally, I spoke. "I think we have to select a Foreman," I said. Again, silence. I turned to a couple of guys who had earlier told me they had served on juries before: "Maybe one of you gentlemen would like to be Foreman," I said. Both shook their heads in a vehement NO!

Then a voice cut in from the head of the table. It was Horace. "Fer chrissake, I've served on six juries!" he barked.

I deferred graciously, "fine," I said, "be my guest."

This is how the battle between Horace and I began. After we unanimously elected him Jury Foreman, his first words were: "All right, this son-of-a-bitch is guilty. Let's get this over with right now. Let's see a show of hands for 'guilty,' right now!"

"Wait a minute! Wait a minute," I said.

Horace whirled.

"I'm not ready," I said.

Horace bowed elaborately, and addressed the rest of the jurors. "Oh," he said, with scathing sarcasm, "he's not ready yet!"

"I'm not sure if he's guilty or not," I said, "I want to hear what the others think before we take a vote."

"Aw fer chrissakes," he sighed deeply, "we got a god-damned bleeding heart here."

I cut in, angry, "never mind that crap, I still want to hear from the others!"

"Well pal, you're gonna have to wait, because I'm calling for a vote right now!"

"Guilty?" The hands went up. "Not guilty?" The hands went up. And guess what? We were split down the middle. Apparently, other jurors had doubts as well.

Horace glared at me again. "Now look what you've done," he snarled thru clenched teeth, "we'll never get outta" here!"

And so it went for two straight days, and we were still deadlocked.

At one point, we were arguing about the defendant's testimony. No one could remember exactly what he had said. So I had to open my mouth again. "We can ask the court clerk to come in and read back the testimony word-for-word, and then we'll know exactly what he said," I suggested.

This unleashed a firestorm from Horace. "I'm the foreman of this jury," he bellowed, "not you!"

"Then be one," I shot back. *"Let's get it right!"*

With a look of pure hatred directed at me, Horace pressed the jury call button, the court stenographer was summoned, she came in, read back the testimony, and we got it right.

That's the way it went between Horace and me. He addressed me in front of all as the "bleeder." I learned later that some of the jurors told him to lay off me, but he didn't and, if anything, his hatred of me increased.

About noon of the second day, we sent word to the Judge that we were deadlocked. The Judge sent word back to try to reach a verdict, and if we were still deadlocked at 2:30 pm, he would reconvene us.

When we reconvened in the courtroom at 2:30 pm we were still deadlocked, so the Judge declared a mistrial and we were free to go.

Horace button-holed me at the top of the stairs; "You bastard!" he snarled, "we could've been outta' there with a guilty verdict in one hour if it hadn't been for you. Instead, it's been two fucking days and we're hung!" Simultaneously, with these words, he took a swing at me. I ducked. He missed, lost his balance, and fell halfway down the stairs. He looked up at me. And I looked down at him, believe it or not, with pity, because I knew that justice had been done.

THE CAPTAIN AND THE SERGEANT

On May 8, 1945, in a tiny schoolhouse in Reims, France, Germany surrendered unconditionally to the Allies, and World War II in Europe was over. But, in the front lines, on both sides, there was confusion. Germany was decimated. Nazis were surrendering by the thousands, and, while we knew the war would end shortly, perhaps in a matter of days, and hours, we did not know exactly when. Thus, we faced a terrible dilemma. How could we avoid getting killed with the end of the war imminent?

This is a story about two young boys; one a Captain and one a Sergeant, caught up in this deadly web. But first, a description of each:

The Captain

Twenty years old. Born Ithaca, New York; West Point graduate, class of 1943; to him, duty, honor, country, are one and the same, a rigid code that has shaped his life. Although his men regard him as an iron-ass, they give him grudging respect. He has led this Company from Normandy, France to the Rhine River, deep in Germany. But, he has one fatal flaw; he cares too much about his men, and in particular:

The Sergeant

Eighteen years old; born Clarkesville, Tennessee; drafted into the infantry in early 1943, high school dropout, handyman, carpenter, drifter; he found a home in the army. Despite his lack of schooling, developed into a fine non-com; highly intelligent, cool, fearless in combat, a born leader, yet he too, like his Captain, has one fatal flaw;

he cares too much about his men. And also, he cares too much about his Captain.

The Scene

The Captain and the Sergeant are crouched in a foxhole, peering through their binoculars at a German town, about a mile away.

"Sergeant!"

"Yes, Sir!"

"Take a recon patrol into the town."

"Yes, sir," the sergeant replied and started to leave.

"Just one minute, Sergeant!"

"Sir?"

"You know the Krauts have lost this war and right now, even as we speak, they're surrendering in some goddam little schoolhouse in France."

"Yes, Sir."

"Now listen, when you take this patrol out, don't, repeat don't try to engage the Krauts. Just reconnoiter, take a look around, then hole up and get your ass back here pronto!"

"Sir?"

"For crissakes Sergeant, do I have to draw a picture for you? We've come a long way, and we've lost a lot of men from this Company. But now, with this fucking war about to end, I don't wanna" lose anymore men! Do you read me?"

"Yes Captain, loud and clear."

"Then get your ass outta" here!"

"Yes, Sir!"

The Captain watched the patrol move out, and advance cautiously toward the town. At this point he realized that he was sweating profusely, fogging his binoculars and trembling uncontrollably.

The patrol disappeared into the town. For an eternity, all was quiet. Then came the crackle of small arms fire, punctuated by the *whamp! whamp!* of hand grenades. He sank to his knees, and he knew despair. Then it was quiet. There was not a sound from the town.

The Captain was beside himself. He could not speak. Terror and guilt laid their cold and heavy hand on him.

For a long time, the Captain crouched, motionless. Then suddenly, he straightened up and clamped the binoculars to his eyes in disbelief. For here came the patrol, in ragged formation, carrying their wounded, staggering, sagging, weaving, until finally, the Sergeant stood before him.

"All prez-han-account fer, Sir!"

The Captain leaned closer to the Sergeant, and he could smell his breath. Then he realized that the Sergeant and the patrol were falling down, limp, giggly, gloriously drunk. No one was wounded. Some were too drunk to stand and had to be carried, that was all. The patrol was intact! Incredulous, the Captain stepped back.

"Hey, Cap," the Sergeant giggled, "we brought cha' somethin'!"

And, as the wobbling, drunken patrol gathered around the Captain in a circle, they deposited at his feet two cases of beer, a bottle of Schnapps, and a huge wheel of German cheese.

"Oh, Cap, I almost forgot. We gotta' couple of Kraut prisoners too." He chortled, jerking his thumb at two terrified German boys, hands locked behind their heads, barely thirteen years old.

"Sergeant," said the Captain.

"Let's you and me take a little walk. And bring some of that Schnapps, and beer, and cheese along too."

"Yes, Sir!"

And so it was
that the Captain and the Sergeant,
sitting with their backs against a haystack,
took a belt of Schnapps,
and another belt,
drank the beer,
hacked off huge chunks of German cheese with their trench knives,
and eventually,
together,
fell asleep in the warm sun
like little boys,
which, of course,
is what they were.

PEARL'S PEOPLE

Prologue

In the summer of 1976, terrorists hijacked an Israeli airliner bound for Tel Aviv from Entebbe, a major city in east Africa. The terrorists aboard ordered the pilot to return to the Entebbe Air Terminal. All 200 Israeli tourists aboard were held hostage in the terminal building.

This act was masterminded by Idi Amin, the Ugandan dictator, who sent word to the Israeli government that unless a specified number of captive terrorists were released by the Israelis, the hostages would be executed every hour on the hour until there were none left alive.

While pretending to consider the terrorist demands, the Israelis, within a 48-hour period, conceived and executed a daring plan to rescue the hostages. Three gigantic Israeli "Hercules" transport airplanes, loaded with paratroopers, were dispatched from Tel Aviv. This strike force flew 1500 miles (the air distance from Los Angeles to Seattle), landing at the Entebbe Air Terminal.

The paratroopers burst from their planes and attacked the terrorist garrison at the terminal. A brief firefight took place. The terrorists were all killed and the hostages were rescued almost intact (one killed). The remaining hostages were flown back to Israel and landed safely at Tel Aviv.

At the time, this brilliantly conceived operation was regarded as a monumental feat of arms. In my opinion, it still is.

When news of the daring Israeli rescue hit the world of television news reporting, it also ricocheted into the programming departments of two television networks. Both ABC and NBC were busting their butts to get on the air ASAP with a docudrama on the rescue.

ABC went to videotape and got on the air first. Shooting started immediately. The first scenes, depicting the planning stages of the operation, were to be shot inside the Federal Building on Wilshire in West Los Angeles. Secondly, the airport battle scenes were to be shot in Stockton, California.

So there I sat on the periphery of all this, snug and bored out of my gourd in my twisted little office on Wilshire Boulevard when the call came in:

"Hello, is this Win Goulden?"

"Yes."

"This is Jim Comisky and I'm recruiting for Pearl's People."

"Pearl's what?"

"Pearl's People, we supply extras for movies and you were recommended to us."

"Me?"

"Yes, you."

"But I've never been in a movie."

"Doesn't matter, no experience is required. We're making a TV docudrama about the Israeli paratrooper's raid on Entebbe. We want you to be an Israeli paratroop colonel."

"Really?"

"So whatta' you say?"

"Okay" (guardedly), "what have I got to lose?"

"Okay, great. Now listen, go to Western Costume for your uniform fitting tomorrow, 8:00 a.m. sharp!"

"Okay, thank you."

"By the way, the shoot pays $25 a day."

When I arrived at Western Costume the next morning, they were ready for me. They whisked me to one of the dressing rooms, then handed me a complete uniform on a coat hanger.

I put everything on and surveyed myself in the mirror. There I stood, clad in the battledress of an Israeli Paratroop Colonel, a fruit salad of ribbons on my chest plus a silver parachute badge as well. I popped on the maroon beret and struck a pose. I looked cool – real cool. The gal assisting me peered at me. "Not bad," she said, "a perfect fit."

"Thank you," I said.

She turned to go, then looked back at me absently and said, "Yum, yum, yummm!"

"I beg your pardon?" I said. But she was gone.

The next morning I drove to the Federal Building on Wilshire Boulevard in West Los Angeles and reported for duty to Jim Cumiskey and his "Pearl's People" clipboard. Trailer dressing rooms, lights and tons of other paraphernalia were rapidly sprouting all over the lawn next to the building; cables, like coiled snakes littered the ground.

Jim directed me to a spot near a trailer. "Wait here," he said.

"What'll I be doing?" I asked.

"I dunno', but they'll call you. Do what they say."

"Okay," I said, and with that I was cut adrift (or so it seemed to me).

There I was, a resplendent Israeli Paratroop Colonel with nothing to do. I stood there awhile and growing bored, strolled over to a seated young lady holding what appeared to be a script. (I learned later that she was a script girl, and maybe a little more, like a Script Supervisor).

"Hi," I said, smiling. She looked up, saw me, ignored me and returned to the script. Not to be put off, I leaned over her. "Is that the script for the movie?" I asked. She looked up at me, incredulous. I blundered on. "I was wondering if you have an extra copy," I said.

She stood up slowly, bowed deeply and with acidic sarcasm said: "Oh, please sir, take mine. I insist!"

I looked into her eyes and saw her contempt. "Is this your first time on a set?" she asked.

"Yes Ma'am."

"Let me give you a little advice Colonel," she sneered, "extras keep their mouths shut, got it? Just park your ass until you're called."

"Yes Ma'am."

She exploded. "Get outta' here and don't call me ma'am!"

"I'm sorry," I said, "evidently I've violated an unwritten code."

"Get out, asshole!" she hissed.

I slunk off, red-faced and crestfallen.

Surveying the set, I saw that crew members were setting up a long table with place settings for the cast and production VIPs. Caterers had arrived and were setting up lunch. I was standing there like a dolt, knowing not what to do when a voice said, "Hello, are you on this shoot?"

I turned, and there stood a very, very young Israeli Paratroop Colonel in full battle dress, identical to mine. He saluted me. "Wait a minute," I said, not wanting this charade to go any further. "I'm not what you think I am," I said. "I'm just an extra and this uniform I'm wearing is from a costume rental company!"

He laughed: "You could have fooled me!" We both laughed. "I'm the military advisor for this shoot," he said.

I interrupted, "Wait a minute; just wait a minute. You were on the actual raid on Entebbe, weren't you?"

"Yes," he said, "my name is Rami." (If he's more than nineteen, I'm a monkey's uncle," I thought).

"Jesus," I said, and began pressing him for details of the actual raid. Before long, still conversing intently, we pulled up two stools. He asked me if I was in World War II. I told him I was a paratrooper and a glider pilot with combat landings in Normandy, Southern France, Holland, Belgium and Germany.

"Wow!" he said. While we were deep in conversation, directly behind us, the cast was sitting down to lunch. "Come on," Rami said.

"Where?"

"You're gonna' have lunch with us!"

"Us?"

"Yeah, you and me, and the cast."

And so it came to pass that I found myself seated between Peter Finch and Jack Warden. Rami introduced me and I found myself the center of the conversation. They, lead by Rami, asked me a million questions about World War II paratroops, and when the lunch concluded, Peter Finch shook my hand. "You must have been crazy," he said.

"I was," I said.

On the way into the Federal Building where the interior shots were to be made, I passed the acidic script girl. She had seen me eating lunch with the cast. Her face was ashen. I extended my arm full length and pointed directly at her. I said, "In the future, young lady, be damned careful how you speak to anyone on any set!"

When we moved from the grounds to shoot interior scenes, all of the extras, including me, moved inside as a group, except that the extras shunned me like the plague. No one would speak to me. Their hate (or fear?) was palpable. I did not know which it was. Once again I had fucked up and done something that irrevocably alienated them. It never occurred to me at that time that maybe the incident with the script girl and the lunch with the stars and cast may have spooked them.

Moving into a large room, I saw a huge table. It was like a giant sand box and an exact scale replica of the Entebbe Airport. Cameras ringed the sandbox and, standing in front of it, clad in Israeli General Staff uniforms were Peter Finch and Jack Warden. I was standing there when Comiskey whispered in my ear, "Go over to the sand table."

"What?"

"You heard me, go on up there, they want you up there!"

"Who?"

"For chrissake," he hissed, "just get up there!"

"Okay, okay."

So while the cameras whirred I stood up there beside Finch, looking down intently at the airport replica, an Israeli Paratroop Colonel on the General Staff.

Not bad for a fifty-seven year old fart, I thought. After the first shoot, Comisky cornered me. "We're going to Stockton for three days to shoot the battle scenes. Do you want to go?"

"No, thanks, Mike," I said. "I appreciate it, but I gotta' go back to work. But will you do me one small favor?"

"Sure."

"Remember that script girl that ripped my ass this morning?"

"Yeah, how could I forget?"

"Give her this note." I pressed a piece of paper into his palm. It said:

"Ma'am: My sincere thanks to you for what you did this morning. Without you, darling, all this would have never happened.
Love, Win Goulden."

SUNDAY

It started out like any other day, but by the time the day ended, my life was changed forever.

It was snowing when I awoke that morning. I arose, shuffled sleepily to the bathroom, brushed my teeth, hit the shower. The wonderful smell of perking coffee, bacon and eggs wafted upstairs to my room like a beckoning finger.

"Breakfast, Winfield," my mother called up from the kitchen. It was Sunday. I was 20 years old.

In the breakfast nook, my mother sat opposite me: "Where's Dad? I asked."

"He had to go over to Gary Raymond's house, their toilet isn't working."

"On Sunday?"

"Yes."

"Why?"

"Because he'll get a little more money if he comes right over now, particularly when it's Sunday."

I went into the living room and snapped on the radio, twiddling the dial to a broadcast of the New York Giants/Brooklyn Dodgers pro football game at Ebbets Field in Brooklyn, New York. The game was tied 7 – 7 late in the fourth quarter.

Then it happened abruptly. "We interrupt this program to bring you this news flash:

PEARL HARBOR HAS BEEN ATTACKED! I repeat: PEARL HARBOR HAS BEEN ATTACKED!"

I leaned closer, second cup of coffee in hand. "Where in the hell is Pearl Harbor?" I thought, irritated that the game had been interrupted.

The announcer continued, "At 8:00am this morning, Honolulu time, Japanese Carrier-based aircraft attacked United States Army and Navy installations at Pearl Harbor on the island of Oahu in Hawaii!"

I sat up straight. Now the announcer had my full attention. I gulped my coffee, listening to the litany of death and disaster:

"Heavy loss of American lives!"

"Battleship Arizona sunk!"

"Hickam Field in flames!"

"Guam, Wake Island, and the Philippines also under attack!"

I took a deep breath. I had been classified one-A in the draft in early June, right after I graduated from Rutgers.

On Monday, December 8, President Roosevelt was on the radio, speaking to the Congress:

"Yesterday, Sunday, December 7th, 1941, a date that will live in infamy, forces of the Japanese Navy and Air Force, suddenly and dastardly attacked United States Army and Navy installations at Pearl Harbor."

Throughout our neighborhood, and throughout the entire nation, all of us were bent over our radios as the fateful words were spoken.

"I ask that the Congress declare that a State of War now exists between the United States and the Japanese Imperial Empire."

I stood up, turning to my parents. "Well," I said, "we're in it now….. and so am I."

On Tuesday, December 9th, I quit my job with the New York Daily News.

On Wednesday, December 10th, I celebrated my 21st birthday.

On Thursday, December 11th, 1941, I enlisted in the United States Army Air Corps.

So began a period in my life when I would experience combat as a paratrooper and glider pilot, fighting in Normandy, Southern France, Holland, Belgium and Germany, and be wounded twice, all in the next five years.

Epilogue

In 1974, I had to make a business trip to Honolulu. When the plane touched down, I didn't immediately head for our Honolulu office. I took the boat trip to Pearl Harbor. I stood on the hull of the overturned battleship Arizona, were 1500 sailors died that terrible December day. I wanted to see where, for me, it all began. And I thought then, as I do now, "Will we ever learn?"

It seems strange now, to be here with hell on earth again, this time in Iraq and Afghanistan. I can only quote to you my feelings of March 2003, when the LA Times ran my letter to the editor:

"To those who would rush to war, are you ready? Are you ready for the body bags that will be flown home, containing the shattered remains of our sons and daughters? Are you ready for the fear, suffering and grief of war? As usual, we old people do the talking and the young do the dying. Be ready."

WEDDING PRESCENCE

It started out like any normal wedding reception, but as the festivities progressed, it became an insane nightmare....for *me*.

This insanity, through a series of unbelievably bizarre mishaps, wrapped its tentacles around me and made me, an innocent guest, the object of disdain and contempt.

Before I go further, let me get into this a little more:

1. My wife's young cousin was getting married. Her wedding took place outdoors at Descanso Gardens, a lovely horticultural jewel placed in the heart of La Canada, California.

2. The reception following the wedding was in an exquisite garden adjacent to the ceremony.

3. Everything was formal, from the men imprisoned in too-tight tuxedos to the young girls clad in flowing gowns to the scooting children, to the aged dowagers with crisp, silver–blue sprayed hairdos and horn-rimmed harlequin glasses. Decorum and correctness prevailed, until I made my debut.

Let me digress again; the reception guests were composed of two groups, WASPS and Italians, co-existing briefly to celebrate this joyous occasion. While the WASPS maintained a silent, almost remote dignity, the Italians joyously started to party immediately, the men shedding their tux jackets as they made a bee-line for the dance floor.

It should also be noted, that while the Italian contingent savored the wine and mellowed out, the WASPS gulped hard booze drinks; all the while looking askance at the Sicilian revelry taking place before their very eyes, until, a short time later, they themselves, in small groups, were carried out on three gurneys, having passed out before the wedding cake was even cut.

So......

I took my lovely, red-headed, drop-dead gorgeous wife in hand and joined the dancers. We started out beautifully, sliding across the dance floor in the first waltz honoring the bride and groom. As we were swooping in a graceful pirouette, I felt a sharp blow on my shoulder, which caused me to lose my balance.

"Hey Win!" the dancer shouted. It was my wife's Uncle Phil, tall, handsome, mustached, the consummate Italian male, a great dancer with the strength of a raging bull.

"Hey Win!" he shouted again, this time giving me a push that (1) catapulted me across the dance floor, knocking down two dancers, and (2) sent me into an uncontrollable slide on my hands and knees that ended with my head buried in the lap of one of the seated, pristine, silver haired dowagers.

Mercifully, I will draw a protective curtain around what took place next. Suffice it to say that after mumbling profuse apologies, as I was retreating in great embarrassment, she was heard to exclaim:

"Disgusting man! He's drunk already, and the reception is just starting!"

A while later, a very, very young beautiful girl approached me with a large circular silver serving tray loaded with flutes of champagne.

"Champagne, sir?" she asked.

"No, thank you," I said, as she extended the tray. At that moment, catastrophe struck. Somehow, as she extended the tray, she tipped it too far forward. We both watched in horror as a waterfall of champagne cascaded and splashed into my lap and I heard the tinkle of broken glass. She stood there for a moment. Then she burst into tears and ran, sobbing, back to the kitchen. By this time, my wet jacket, shirt and trousers stank with the cloying sweet-n-sour smell of flat champagne, and to put it mildly, my cool was shattered.

I rose from the table and hung my drenched jacket over the back of an empty chair, and at this time, I made a major decision:

"Fuck it," I thought, "I'm gonna' have fun in spite of all this crap!"

I rose from the table and walked to the dance floor, found a partner and started to dance. The band kicked off a blues in jump-tempo and I took off with my partner and for about three minutes we had the floor to ourselves. Every swing dance step I ever knew (both of them) I put together with my partner in a wild and frenetic whirl. People formed a circle around us, clapping enthusiastically (that is to say, the Italians did).

Flushed and triumphant, I returned to my seat, twisting slightly to the right to talk to my wife.

"You look cute," she said.

"What!?"

"Sexy."

"Are you out of your mind?"

"No," she said, "just horny."

Since this is the best conversation any man, or woman, married or single can ever have, I leaned forward to kiss her. Unaware, at that precise moment, that someone had set a cup of hot coffee at my elbow. Of course, when I turned, guess what? Did it splash on the table? No, of course not; it flowed gently up the sleeve of my shirt, all the way to my armpit!

After the scalding subsided, I slumped back in my chair, utterly defeated.

The final insult, however, was yet to come.

Preparing to leave, I reached for my jacket which, you will recall, I had draped over the back of a chair. I picked it up and shrugged into it; *too small.*

"This jacket isn't mine," I sighed. Sure enough it didn't fit. Some jerk had made off with mine.

The next day my wife was on the phone with her cousin, the father of the bride.

"It was a great wedding!" he said.

"Yes, it was great," my wife replied, "except for what happened to Win."

"Well everything went perfect, so thank Win for being the recipient of the only negative things that happened," he chuckled.

I grabbed the phone. "Tell me about it," I snarled, seeing again that blue-haired old woman nodding knowingly.

The irony of all this is that I was and am a recovered alcoholic and have been sober for 40 years.

SYLVIA

The light burns late
In her studio
A place
Of happy chaos
And bleak despair
Womb of creativity
Hope
Fears
Triumph
Tears

For she is caught up
In the bitter-sweet pain of creation
Birth pangs
The heights
The depths
Her senses
Dulled
By fatigue

Her insecurities
Flash like turn signals
Angels of hope
Intervene
And

Yet again
The journey is renewed

The days march by
On leaden feet
Darkness
Fear of failure
Lurks

But then
At last
The creation
Is birthed
In brightest light
And now
Seen by different eyes
She feels
Redemption
And sweet release

STOMACH MUSCLES

The dance pavilion at Roton Point Park stood tall, its stilt-like piles extending on tiptoe into the placid waters of Long Island Sound. Its Marquee blinked brightly, each week heralding the appearance of yet another swing band of the thirties. Japanese lanterns, strung from invisible overhead wires, shed a phantasmagoria of brilliant red, blue, orange and gold light.

In the peripheral darkness, under the massive oak trees that dotted the park, fireflies winked magically. Over it all, like a perfumed shroud, hung the smell of grilling hot dogs, sizzling hamburgers, peanuts, cotton candy and salt water taffy.

It was the summer of 1934. I was in my early teens. And I was quite drunk – drunk with my love of jazz, and also, drunk with the realization that tonight, of all nights, I was going to see, and hear, in person, the great Louis Armstrong, his trumpet, and his band.

I also had a mission. I regularly wrote a jazz column for my high school newspaper, and tonight, I was determined to interview the great one. When the band took a break after the first set, I headed for the bus, pencil behind my ear and notepad in hand. I tapped on the door, peering through the glass:

"Mr. Armstrong, Mr. Armstrong," I quavered.

Then suddenly from nowhere, a voice barked, "Scram kid, get the hell outta" here!"

Then Louis looked up. Our eyes locked. And to this day, I don't know why, but he growled, in that wonderful gravel voice, "Let the kid in!"

I pushed the door open, and there he was, sitting behind the empty driver's seat, his silver trumpet at his side. He looked tired and he was sweating. He turned to me, and his eyes were gentle. "Kid, what do you want?"

Pad and pencil poised, I blurted, "Mr. Armstrong, my name is Winfield Goulden. I write a jazz column for my high school newspaper and I want to interview you!"

"All right, kid."

Scared shitless, I plunged on. "Mr. Armstrong, I read that you once hit 100 high C's on your trumpet, followed by a high F. Is that true?"

His white teeth shone. "Well, I'll be damned. Now how in the hell did you know that?"

The ice was broken, and from then on the interview flowed smoothly from question to answer to question to answer. I had done my homework. I had done my research. I knew every record he had made, the personnel, the recording date......everything.

He was impressed. I was in euphoria. Finally, I repeated my original question: "How can you hit such high notes on your trumpet? How can you hit F above high C so many times?"

There was a pause. Then he turned and said, "Stomach muscles."

When my high school paper ran the interview, I sent a copy to Louis Armstrong. A week later I received a large envelope in the mail. It was from him. It was an autographed 8 x 10 glossy photo. It was personally signed by Louis Armstrong. It said:

"To the kid who knows more about me than I do."

And below his signature he had also written *"Stomach Muscles."*

WINTER DREAMS II

Park Bench

Prologue

Picture
New York City
In winter

Picture
A bench in Central Park
A soft
Gentle
Snow is falling

This tale
Is about
Some of the people
That occupied this bench
In a three-hour span
One winter's day

PARK BENCH

A young man
And a young woman
Sit together
Clutching
In passionate embrace
Pressing
Caressing
Shutting out the world
With their ardor
The snow flakes too
Caress their hands
And lips
And hearts
So long have they pressed together
That the snow
Has placed its mantle on them
And they are one

*

A young boy
With eyes of mischief
Turned up nose
Wool skating cap
With top knot
Jack Frost nips

His skates click
A metallic sound
A bandolier
About his neck
Harbinger
Of joyous day
Yet to come

For a time
He sits
With upturned face
A mask of purest white
Caroling
Caroling
In his heart
For the joyous day
Yet to come

*

A young mother
Sits
Gingerly
With
Happy fatigue

Her children squirming puppies
Wriggle and giggle
With laughter's warmth

Oh
Sing my song
Of love lasting
Daughter of Eve

*

The soldier sits stiffly
In his teens
Braced
At attention
Ribbons on his chest
Attest
Bone-aching fatigue
Weariness

Fear and grief
Draw him to hunched position
A young man
With an old man's eyes

For he has seen
Far too much
Yet not enough
For the high noon
Of his youth
Is forever gone
And now
He sees
Only twilight

*

And then another man
Manic
Satanic
Newspaper folded
And clutched

His hands tremble
His doom
Reverberating
With ticker tape
And trash

For he lives on the farthest rim
A land of woe
And
What might have been

Ignorant
Of winter's caress
Eyes wide shut

With nothingness

*

An old man
And an old woman
Sit together
Enfolded in tender embrace
Touching gently
With the respect
Of many years
Earned
And deserved

The whole world
Shut out
By their need
Each for the other

So long have they pressed together
That the snow
Now has wrapped its mantle
Completely around them
And they are one
Forever

Epilogue

The bench
Once more
Is clear
Time passes
But another day
Is coming
To accommodate
More asses

CPSIA information can be obtained at www.ICGtesting.com
Printed in the USA
LVOW082239190312

273800LV00001B/7/P